FLORIDA SPORTS TRIVIA

**Ed Maloney
and
J. Alexander Poulton**

2011 by OverTime Books
First printed in 2011 10 9 8 7 6 5 4 3 2 1
Printed in Canada

All rights reserved. No part of this work covered by the copyrights hereon may be reproduced or used in any form or by any means—graphic, electronic or mechanical—without the prior written permission of the publisher, except for reviewers, who may quote brief passages. Any request for photocopying, recording, taping or storage on information retrieval systems of any part of this work shall be directed in writing to the publisher.

The Publisher: OverTime Books is an imprint of Éditions de la Montagne Verte

Library and Archives Canada Cataloguing in Publication

Maloney, Ed, 1961–
    Florida sports trivia / Ed Maloney, J. Alexander Poulton.

ISBN 978-1-897277-60-7

    1. Sports—Florida—Miscellanea. I. Poulton, J. Alexander (Jay Alexander), 1977– II. Title.

GV584.F5M35 2011   796.09759   C2010-907614-4

Project Director: J. Alexander Poulton
Cover Images: marathon runner, © 2010 Thinkstock/Photodisc; jai alai, © 2010 Thinkstock/Ryan McVay; sail surfer, © Hemera Technologies; Miami Dolphin Sun Life Stadium, © Sun Life; NASCAR racecar, © Lawrence Weslowski Jr. I Dreamstime.com; speedboat, © Joe Stone/Dreamstime.com; horse race, © 2006 Kevin Taylor/Jupiterimages; golfer, © iStockphoto.com/Sergey Kashkin; football, © Toddtaulman/Dreamstime.com; baseball glove, © Bobbiholmes/Dreamstime.com; boxing gloves, © Zedcor Wholly Owned; all other images, © Photos.com

We acknowledge the financial support of the Government of Canada through the Book Publishing Industry Development Program (BPIDP) for our publishing activities.

 Canadian Heritage   Patrimoine canadien

Table of Contents

Introduction **6**

Chapter 1:
Old Traditions **8**

Chapter 2:
Fins, Bucs and Jags **40**

Chapter 3:
The Great American Race **97**

Chapter 4:
Homegrown Highlights **108**

Chapter 5:
Success on Ice Melts Floridians' Hearts **120**

Chapter 6:
Heat, Magic and King James **132**

Chapter 7:
The Net, the Ring, the Ponies and the Superstars . **141**

Chapter 8:
Floridians Who Left Their Mark **168**

Chapter 9:
Florida Sports Hall of Fame Members **201**

Notes on Sources **212**

Dedication

To Arthur Maloney, Kathryn Ryan, Dennis O'Shea and Juliana Cronin. A century ago, they left behind their families and friends on the Emerald Isle to pursue their hopes and dreams in the New World. Also to their children, especially Edward Maloney and Patricia O'Shea; my siblings, Mary, Kathleen and Richard; and my godmother, Margret-Ann Maloney, whose sacrifice, love, devotion and encouragement have allowed me to pursue mine.

– Ed Maloney

To my grandmother, Cynthia Roach

– J. Alexander Poulton

Acknowledgments

I've benefited from the professionalism, mentoring and friendship of scores of individuals in my career as a writer, editor and online producer, especially at *Newsday*, *The Ring* magazine and CBS SportsLine. My eternal thanks to Mike Acri; John and Maureen Andrias; Dotty Beekman; Ed Brophy; Arlen D. "Spider" Bynum; Mike Candel; Bob Cassidy; Leon Carter; Eric Compton; Steve Farhood; Thomas Hayes; Dave Kaplan; Hank Kaplan; Joe Kelly; John Q. Kelly; Ed McNamara; Don Majeski; Arthur Maloney, PhD; Captain Richard J. Maloney, FDNY, Ret.; Kevin Mattimore; Tony Mauro; Arthur Mercante Sr.; John Quinn; Gerry Monigan; Francis Romano; Dave Rubinstein; Evan Rudowski; Jeff Ryan; Stu Saks; Pete Tamburello; Manny Topol and John Truehart.

A tip of the hat goes to Joe Pauly and Frank and Denise Maloney for their critique and review of early versions of the manuscript. And I am extremely grateful for the professionalism and dedication of the editorial staff at OverTime Books. Because of my love of sports and history, I knew this assignment would be extremely rewarding. I was not disappointed.

– *Ed Maloney*

Introduction

As our lives progress, we realize that some moments that were considered ordinary have taken on a whole new dimension or become of greater importance, in a historical context, as we look back across the veil of years. When the Brooklyn Dodgers left New York for Los Angeles in 1958, one of the local papers listed the top 10 highlights of the team's stay in New York. Jackie Robinson's breaking the color barrier was not even listed. Today, it's considered one of the major sporting events of the 20th century.

Those people who are old enough to remember can easily recall where they were and what they were doing when they heard of President Kennedy's assassination or when Neil Armstrong first set foot on the moon. Recalling these remarkable events and the people and circumstances surrounding them falls into the category of trivia. That's especially true when the subject turns to sports. Even your average sports fan can easily recall where they were and who they were with when their team won a championship or upset a hated rival. They also remember those same details surrounding agonizing defeats. Try telling them it's *just* a game or, if you're really brave, that it's trivial.

In the pages that follow, we will look back at some of the memorable sporting events that took place in Florida—noteworthy personalities and the accomplishments and milestones of native Floridians—as well as special moments of the professional teams and the universities that call the Sunshine State home. This is not a history of Florida sports or its great athletes, nor does it attempt to be. Rather, it's a collection of facts and anecdotes with some bits and pieces of uncommon knowledge that we hope you have as much fun reading as we did discovering during our research and writing.

Chapter One

Old Traditions

It wasn't until the early 1950s that Florida State joined the universities of Florida and Miami as the Sunshine State's representatives in Division I football. But there was one huge problem—the three teams seldom cracked the national top 20 rankings. And the latter two programs had been around for decades before the Seminoles upgraded their program in 1954.

But that all changed when Bobby Bowden took over the reins at FSU in 1976. He quickly turned the program around and made the Seminoles consistent winners. Three years later, Howard Schnellenberger rescued a losing Miami program from the brink of being canceled and went on to win a national championship in 1983.

With the ascension of their two in-state rivals' programs to national prominence, the Gator Nation demanded the same. And they've had it on a pretty consistent basis since Steve Spurrier returned to Gainesville to coach at his alma mater in 1990. All three schools were proud of their distinct traditions, but now they had one in common—they were all national champions.

University of Florida Gators
Nothing But Excellence

Jack Youngblood was a dominating football player at every level of organized competition he played, from high school through college to the NFL. He was a two-way player and team captain at Monticello-Jefferson County High School in Monticello. The future Pro Football Hall of Famer earned All-State honors leading a defense that shut out seven opponents in 12 games en route to winning the 1966 state championship.

Youngblood was named to Florida's All-Time High School Football Team by *Sports Illustrated* in 1989. In November 2007, he was voted to the Florida High School Athletic Association's All-Century High School football team. At the University of Florida, he was moved to the defensive line, and by his senior year, he had developed into an All-American. That same season, he was named the Most Valuable Defensive Lineman in the Southeast Conference and was also a finalist for the Outland Trophy, which is given to the nation's best college lineman.

In 1969, Youngblood was part of a 9–1–1 Gator team that upset the University of Tennessee Volunteers in the Gator Bowl in Ray Graves' final game as coach at the University of Florida. Youngblood played a key role in that bowl game, recording nine tackles and forcing a fumble. Earlier that season, he gained national attention after a five-sack performance in a win over Florida State.

The Rip, Strip and Grip

In 1970, Jack Youngblood made one of the most famous plays in Gator history. Leading the Gators 17–10 with five minutes left to play, the University of Georgia Bulldogs were on the Florida two-yard line, threatening to put the game away. Youngblood stopped running back Ricky Lake short of the end zone, forced a fumble and then made the recovery. That changed the momentum of the game, and the Gators went on to score two touchdowns and win 24–17. The play became known as the "Rip, Strip and Grip." The Gators were 28–12–2 during Youngblood's stay in Gainesville.

A Legend Gets Traded and Another Is Created

The then–Los Angeles Rams selected Youngblood in the first round (20th pick overall) of the 1971 NFL Draft. When future Hall of Fame defensive end Deacon Jones missed a few games with an injury, Youngblood stepped in and made an immediate impact, eventually making the All-Rookie team. The Rams were so impressed with Youngblood's rookie campaign that they decided to trade Jones the next year.

Playing his whole career for the Rams, Youngblood benefited from the mentoring of Jones and another future Hall of Famer, defensive tackle Merlin Olsen. By 1973, Youngblood was a full-time starter and began a string of seven consecutive Pro Bowl seasons. During that time, he was named NFL Defensive Lineman of the Year (1975) and NFC Defensive Player of the Year (1976).

Youngblood's reputation for toughness and durability was forever sealed during the 1979 playoffs. Against Dallas in the divisional round, he fractured his left fibula during a grueling battle with perennial All-Pro and future Hall of Fame tackle, Rayfield Wright. Despite the injury, Youngblood not only finished the Dallas game, but he also continued to play, with the aid of a fitted brace, through the playoffs and into the Super Bowl against Pittsburgh.

"Jack doesn't have a high threshold of pain; he has no threshold at all," Rams trainer Gary Tuthill remarked. It's not surprising that among the many accolades given Youngblood, one coach called him "the John Wayne" of the NFL.

Success in Sports Translates to Victory on the Battlefield

At the turn of the last century, a young West Point cadet named Douglas MacArthur coined the phrase, "Upon the fields of friendly strife are sown the seeds that, upon other fields, on other days, will bear the fruits of victory." That phrase became popular and was eventually engraved on the wall inside one of the academy's athletic buildings.

Those words have been inspirational for thousands of cadets throughout the years, including James Van Fleet, a Bartow native who was a standout fullback on the 1914 Army football team. His graduating class of 1915 later became known as "the class the stars fell on." One of his classmates, a tough farm boy from Kansas named Dwight Eisenhower, had his football career cut short because of a knee injury. Another, Omar Bradley, excelled as a baseball player. But Eisenhower and Bradley were just two of the 59 graduates that year who would rise to the rank of general in the military.

After serving in World War I, Van Fleet stayed in the army and had a series of assignments, including ROTC instructor at the University of Florida. Because of his fame as a football player and his bearing as a combat infantry officer, the 31-year-old Van Fleet was offered the head coaching job at UF in 1923. In his two seasons at the helm, Van Fleet led the Gators to 6–1–2 and 6–2–2 records, respectively.

Van Fleet stayed in the army until 1953 and eventually attained the rank of four-star general. During World War II, he served under General George Patton (a 1912 Olympian) during the Allies' liberation of France and Germany in 1944–45. In 1946, he was sent to Greece to help quell the civil war and administer "the Truman Doctrine."

His success in Greece was so appreciated that a statue of Van Fleet stands in the central town square of the Greek city of Kastoria. He also served in the Korean War, first as commanding general of the U.S. Second Army and later replacing General Matthew Ridgeway as commander of the U.S. Eighth Army and all the United Nations forces in Korea when Ridgeway was promoted following General MacArthur's dismissal by President Truman.

When Van Fleet retired in 1953, Truman said that he ranked among America's greatest generals. His citations for gallantry include three Distinguished Service Crosses (the nation's second highest award for valor), three Silver Stars, three Bronze Stars and three Purple Hearts.

Van Fleet, whose life as a soldier, statesman, athlete and coach epitomized MacArthur's famous phrase, died in 1992 at his ranch in Polk City at age 100. In 1998, a panel of Florida historians and other consultants named Van Fleet one of the 50 most important Floridians of the 20th century.

Here Comes the Judge

Before his stint at the University of Florida, James Van Fleet was an ROTC instructor and assistant football coach at the University of Kansas. One of the better players on the Jayhawks squad during that time was Harold Sebring, who, like his coach, was a decorated combat veteran of World War I.

Van Fleet was reassigned to UF in 1921, where again his duties included coaching the football team. When Sebring graduated in 1923, Van Fleet offered him a coaching position in Gainesville. Sebring also used the opportunity to enroll in law school.

When Van Fleet was reassigned following the 1924 season, Sebring took over his position as Gators coach. In three seasons under Sebring, the team's record was 17–11–2, but he resigned following the 1927 season to concentrate on his law career. It should be noted that the players Sebring recruited went 8–1 in 1928, followed by an 8–2 campaign in 1929.

With football behind him, Sebring remained in Florida to practice law. In 1933, he was appointed a State Circuit Court judge and served in that position until he was named to the Florida Supreme Court in 1943.

Sebring established an excellent reputation on the bench and received a presidential appointment by Harry Truman to serve as a judge at the Nuremberg Trials of Nazi war criminals in 1946 and 1947. After Nuremberg, he returned to the Florida Supreme Court, where he was chief justice from 1951 to 1953. He retired from the Florida bench in 1955 to become the dean of the Stetson University College of Law and remained at Stetson until his death in 1968.

A Star on Both Field and Screen

Dale Van Sickel was a local football star at Gainesville High School and was recruited to UF by coach Harold Sebring. He was a three-year starter at right end from 1927 to 1929, and in 1928, he became the first player to earn first-team All-American honors. The 1928 Gators finished 8–1 and outscored opponents 366–44 to lead the nation in scoring.

Van Sickel was hampered by injuries in his senior season, but he still managed to earn second-team All-American honors. The team went 23–6 in his three years under coach Charlie Bachman. Van Sickel, who was inducted into the College Football Hall of Fame in 1975, was also the team captain for the basketball and baseball teams. The two-time All-American graduated in 1930 and remained in Gainesville as an assistant basketball and football coach for the Gators in 1930–31.

Van Sickel then moved to Hollywood and began a career as a stuntman in the movies. Over the next four decades, he made more than 400 appearances as an actor or stuntman in television and motion pictures. He was a stunt double in major productions that starred actors such as John Wayne and Clarke Gable.

One of Van Sickel's early onscreen appearances was in the 1933 Marx Brothers movie *Duck Soup*, and one of the last movies he appeared in was the Disney classic *The Love Bug* in 1968. Some of the more notable films in which he appeared are *The Greatest Show on Earth*, *Jim Thorpe: All-American* and *The Fighting Kentuckian*.

Van Sickel was a founding member and the first president of the Stuntmen's Association of Motion Pictures. He died in 1977, at age 69, as a result of injuries received while filming a car crash stunt two years earlier.

From Local to State to National Hero

Walter "Tiger" Mayberry was a three-year starter on poor Gators teams in the late 1930s. The Daytona Beach native was a local football phenom on both sides of the ball, as well as an excellent punter. Perhaps the biggest highlight of his career came in 1937, when he led the Gators to their first win over Georgia, 6–0.

In Gainesville, Mayberry attained two distinctions: he was the first player named All-SEC (1937), and he was also the first University of Florida player drafted by the NFL—he was chosen by the Cleveland Rams.

When World War II broke out, Mayberry joined the Marines and became a fighter pilot. Stationed in the South Pacific, he was credited with four kills (five were needed to be considered an "ace"), and he had four more listed as "probable" when he was shot down in a dogfight with the Japanese on August 30, 1943.

Mayberry was captured soon after and sent to the notorious POW camp on the island of Rabaul. He was murdered in captivity, as was fellow UF alumnus Henry Keel, an army air force officer who was on the boxing team during his years at Gainesville.

An Enduring Symbol of Courage and Character

Forrest "Fergie" Ferguson followed Mayberry as a two-way standout for the Gators and became only the second Gator to be named All-American. The Stuart native was a two-sport star at UF and is a member of the Florida Sports Hall of Fame. He was named All-SEC in each of the three years he played football and was the 1942 national AAU javelin champ.

The highlight of Ferguson's stay at Gainesville came in 1941, when he scored the only two touchdowns in a 14–0 win over Miami. He graduated from UF in 1942, and soon afterward, he joined the army and was commissioned a second lieutenant.

On D-Day, Ferguson led his platoon ashore on Omaha Beach during the invasion of Normandy. With his men pinned down by enemy machine-gun fire, Ferguson rose and cleared a passage for his men using a Bangalore torpedo and was gravely wounded leading the assault against the enemy.

He was awarded the Distinguished Service Cross for his heroism, but he never fully recovered from his wounds and died in 1954 at age 34. Since 1954, the University of Florida has given the Forrest K. (Fergie) Ferguson Award to the "senior football player who displays outstanding leadership, character and courage." Some of the more noteworthy recipients have included Steve Spurrier, Jack Youngblood, John Reaves, Wes Chandler, Neal Anderson and Louis Murphy.

He Walked the Walk Before He Talked the Talk

Before becoming an award-winning broadcaster, Cris Collinsworth made his reputation catching the football for the Florida Gators of the late 1970s. From 1977 to 1980, Collinsworth was a three-time All-SEC and two-time All-American wide receiver. He caught 120 passes for 1937 yards and 14 touchdowns. He also ran for two other touchdowns and returned a kickoff for another score. He was inducted into the Verizon Academic All-America Hall of Fame in 2001.

Collinsworth, who was born in Dayton, Ohio, moved to Titusville with his family as a child and went on to graduate from Astronaut High School there. His career at Florida was good enough to warrant being drafted by the Cincinnati Bengals in the second round of the 1981 draft. Collinsworth justified that selection by earning three trips to the Pro Bowl during an eight-year career that included starting on Cincinnati's two Super Bowl teams, in 1981 and 1988.

Record-setting Touchdown Pass

Before Collinsworth established himself as one of the top receivers in Florida history, he made the record books during his freshman year on the initial end of a scoring pass. In a 1977 game against Rice in Houston, Collinsworth connected with receiver Derrick Gaffney on an NCAA record 99-yard touchdown pass in a 48–3 win over the Owls.

Ker's Winghouse

Crawford Ker didn't start playing football until his senior year at Dunedin High School. Even though the Dunedin Falcons won a county championship, Ker didn't receive any scholarship offers, so he enrolled at Arizona Western Junior College in Yuma, Arizona, where he became a Junior College All-American offensive lineman.

He was then offered a scholarship to play football at the University of Florida, where he became a starter and member of the "Great Wall of Florida," which also featured Phil Bromley, Lomas Brown, Billy Hinson and Jeff Zimmerman. The unit protected quarterback Kerwin Bell and opened up holes for running backs John L. Williams and Neal Anderson. The 1984 team finished 9–1–1, and the Gators won their first Southeastern Conference championship.

This son of Scottish immigrants (at one point, his father was a guard at Buckingham Palace) was drafted in 1985 by the NFL in the third round by the Dallas Cowboys. Ker quickly became a starter and played for the Cowboys through 1990. He left Dallas via free agency and had brief stints with Denver and Detroit, but while in Big D, Ker opened holes for running backs Tony Dorsett and Emmitt Smith and helped protect quarterback Troy Aikman, all of whom are in the Pro Football Hall of Fame.

After retiring from football in 1992, Ker ventured into the restaurant business. After a rocky start, he opened Ker's Winghouse Bar & Grill in Largo in 1994. Since then, Ker has added 18 more locations throughout Central Florida, from the Tampa Bay area through Orlando to Daytona Beach.

Number 22 Was Number 1
Wherever He Played

Emmitt Smith's accomplishments on the football field left observers speechless at every level he played. He capped his record-setting career at Escambia High School in Pensacola by being named the top prep player in the country by *USA Today* and *Parade* magazine.

He then quickly established himself as the best running back to ever call the "Swamp" home. When Smith left the University of Florida following his junior year, he owned 58 school rushing records, including most yards in a career (3928), most yards in a season (1599), most yards in a single game (316), most career touchdowns (36) and longest run (96).

At five feet, nine inches and 210 pounds, most NFL scouts thought that Smith was too small to survive long in the pros. The New York Jets were one of the teams that agreed, and they selected Penn State's Blair Thomas second overall in the 1990 draft. Smith would have to wait until the 17th pick before he was drafted by the Dallas Cowboys, who were coming off a 1–15 season.

The experts were dead wrong, as Blair never rushed for more than 728 yards in any of his six seasons. All Smith did en route to the Pro Football Hall of Fame was play in eight Pro Bowls, win four rushing titles, play on three Super Bowl championship teams and become the all-time leading rusher in NFL history, with 18,355 yards.

A Late Start, But a Strong Finish

Emmitt Smith missed the first two games of the 1993 season because of a contract holdout. When he rejoined the defending champion Cowboys, they were 0–2 and in panic mode. With Dallas, Smith went on to win his third consecutive rushing title—despite missing those first two games—and win the Most Valuable Player award for the regular season and Super Bowl XXVIII.

Smith grabbed post-career glory in a similar manner when he won the *Dancing with the Stars* competition in 2006. Despite low scores from the three-judge panel in the early rounds of the hit ABC television show, Smith and partner Cheryl Burke finished strong and bested an 11-couple field that included country singer Sara Evans and television host Jerry Springer. To date, he is the only professional athlete to have won the competition.

Millions Benefit from Revolutionary Drink

The Gatorade shower, in which a victorious football team douses their coach with a cooler filled with the sports drink Gatorade as the final seconds tick off the clock, has become a ritual in championship games at virtually every level of football. But the drink's invention served a far more useful purpose.

As late as the mid-1960s, football players were expected to endure preseason summer practices in the intense summer heat. Drinking water was frowned upon because it could cause cramps. Occasionally, you might read about a player, even a high school player, who had died from dehydration or a stroke.

That all began to change in 1965, when University of Florida assistant football coach Dewayne Douglas approached Dr. James Cade, who at the time ran the College of Medicine's renal and electrolyte division at the university, and inquired why players were sweating and losing so much weight but not urinating.

After the meeting with Douglas, Cade, along with colleagues Dana Shires, Jim Free and A.M. deQuesada, started thinking about the effects of heat on the human body. The team realized that all that sweat was taking with it the players' energy, strength and endurance. The researchers speculated that the body's delicate chemical balance was being upset by the loss of electrolytes, primarily sodium and potassium, in the players' sweat.

To test their findings, Cade approached Douglas' boss, head coach Ray Graves, about letting him use several players as test subjects. Graves agreed, but insisted that the guinea pigs would be the freshman team, not the varsity players.

The findings from this controlled study were shocking. After playing in the heat, the players' electrolytes were completely out of balance and their blood sugar was low, as was their total blood volume. The impact on the body of this upheaval in chemistry was profound.

"Each of these conditions, by itself, would to some extent incapacitate a player," Cade said in an interview for the university's Oral History Project in 1996. "Put them all together, and you can have real problems."

With hard data in hand, Cade's team began pursuing a remedy to address all these issues.

"The solution," Cade said, "was to give them water, but with salt in it to replace the salt they were losing in sweat. Also, give them sugar to keep their blood sugar up, but not so much sugar that it would upset their stomachs."

By all accounts, the first batch of the new electrolyte-replacement drink tasted so bad that none of the scientists could stomach it. Thankfully, Cade's wife suggested adding lemon juice—and Gatorade was born.

The new drink was then given to some squads of Florida players during scrimmages. Nobody was surprised when the players drinking Gatorade fared considerably better than those who didn't as the scrimmage progressed in the intense Florida heat.

Graves witnessed this and had Cade's team produce enough Gatorade for Florida's next game, which was against heavily favored Louisiana State. Florida came from behind in the second half, played in 102-degree heat and beat the Tigers 14–7.

Beginning in 1966, an ample supply of the drink was made for each game, and the Gators went on to finish the season 9–2, which included a 27–12 win over Georgia Tech in the Orange Bowl on New Year's Day 1967. By now, Graves was speaking openly about the beneficial effects of Gatorade, and at the end of the season, the university released an official statement. Their secret was out.

As hard as it may be to believe, Cade was rebuffed when he approached school officials about marketing Gatorade. However, they did change their minds a few years after Cade sold the formula to an Indiana-based company, Stokely-Van Camp. The university claimed that the royalties that Cade and his associates were being paid belonged to the school and sued them. It took more than two years for a settlement to be reached.

Gatorade was later sold to Quaker Oats, which eventually merged with PepsiCo, but the original formula has changed very little over the years. The company maintains that its blend of carbohydrates (sucrose, glucose and fructose) and electrolytes (potassium and sodium) is the optimal mixture for stimulating fluid absorption, helping the body maintain fluid balance, providing energy to working muscles and enhancing athletic performance.

Cade, who died in 2007 at age 80, did not rest on his Gatorade laurels. He continued to work at the University of Florida in endeavors to improve the human condition. Some of his inventions and ideas included the first shock-dissipating football helmet, a high-protein milkshake used by surgical patients, athletes and cancer patients, and a method for treating autism and schizophrenia through diet modification. Researchers are continuing his autism research at the J. Robert Cade Foundation in Cordoba, Argentina, using much of Dr. Cade's data and equipment.

University of Miami Hurricanes

It's Always Darkest Before the Dawn

The Miami Hurricanes have won more national championships than any other Division I program since they capped their miracle 1983 season with a win over Nebraska at the Orange Bowl. But few people remember how close the university came to dropping the program to Division I-AA status and even cancelling football completely in the 1970s.

The post George Mira–Ted Hendricks eras of the 1960s saw losing season after losing season become a losing decade. From 1969 to 1978, UM was 41–67, and the football team had finished in the top 20 only once since 1957. At the same time, Don Shula had turned the once-hapless Dolphins of the NFL into consistent winners. Football-crazy fans were filling the Orange Bowl, but it was on Sunday afternoons, not Saturdays.

It was decided to give the program one last chance to regain a modicum of respectability. The task was given to a man who had never been a head coach at the college level, and his one full season in the NFL had ended 4–10. When Howard Schnellenberger arrived on the Coral Gables campus in 1979, the Hurricanes had had a losing record in eight of their last 10 seasons and hadn't won a bowl game since 1966.

One of the first things the new coach did was aggressively recruit more local players, developing the "State of Miami" concept. From his years with the Dolphins, Schnellenberger knew that South Florida had a deep reservoir of football talent, but the area was being harvested by the rest of the nation.

Although the Canes were 5–6 in 1979, they were a better team and turned the corner in 1980 with a 9–3 record, the first of 17 consecutive winning seasons. Miami ended the 1980 and 1981 seasons ranked 18th and eighth, respectively, by the Associated Press. The Hurricanes under Schnellenberger had become a national program. His next goal was winning a national championship.

Canes Recruited Future Coach

Schnellenberger had just one full season's experience as a head coach, but he did have an impressive résumé. The Louisville, Kentucky, native was recruited to play college ball at Miami in 1952. He liked South Florida and was prepared to play for coach Andy Gustafson, but the coach of the University of Kentucky also wanted the local star. The UK coach even brought the governor to Schnellenberger's home to attempt to persuade the player and his parents. When that didn't work, the persistent Wildcats coach then found out that the Schnellenbergers were devout Catholics and was able to land his prized recruit with the help of the

Archbishop of Louisville. The coach's name was Paul "Bear" Bryant.

After earning All-American honors as an end at Kentucky, Schnellenberger played a few years in the Canadian Football League (CFL) before returning to his alma mater in 1959 to become an assistant coach under Blanton Collier. Another assistant coach on Collier's staff was Don Shula. Then Schnellenberger joined Bryant's staff at Alabama during the Crimson Tide's three national championships in the early 1960s; he made the jump to the NFL and did four years under George Allen in Los Angeles before reuniting with Shula in Miami from 1970 to 1972. After a disastrous stint as the head coach with the Baltimore Colts in 1973, Schnellenberger rejoined Shula's staff, where he stayed until he took the UM job.

The Game of Games

When Schnellenberger took the reins at Miami, he wasn't going to settle for just making the program competitive—he wanted to win a national championship. But the goal of playing in the ultimate bowl game in January didn't appear realistic after his team was thoroughly thrashed 28–3 by the Gators in the 1983 season opener.

Under freshman quarterback Bernie Kosar, Miami reeled off 10 consecutive wins, including a 17–16 victory over Florida State in the regular season finale in Tallahassee. When the bowl bids were announced, the number five ranked Canes drew an invitation to the Orange Bowl, where they'd be facing the

Nebraska Cornhuskers, who were rated number one in the preseason and maintained that ranking by dominating most of their opponents en route to a 12–0 record.

The 50th Orange Bowl, played on January 2, 1984, is still regarded as the best. Earlier in the day, number two ranked Texas was upset by Georgia in the Cotton Bowl, and number three Auburn was unimpressive in its win over Michigan in the Sugar Bowl. So it was possible, though highly unlikely, that Miami could leapfrog from number five to number one. All UM had to do was beat the team that was regarded as one of the best in Division I history.

With their pro-style passing attack, the 11-point underdog Canes jumped to a 17–0 lead on a pair of touchdown passes from Kosar to Glenn Dennison and a 45-yard field goal by kicker Jeff Davis.

Nebraska got its running game on track, led by Heisman Trophy–winning running back Mike Rozier, and answered with two touchdowns, trailing 17–14 at halftime. After Nebraska tied the score at 17 early in the second half, Kosar engineered two touchdown drives that culminated with runs by Alonzo Highsmith and Albert Bentley to give Miami a 31–17 lead late in the third quarter.

Quarterback Turner Gill rallied Nebraska with a touchdown drive that ended with Jeff Smith's one-yard run with 6:55 left in the fourth quarter to cut Miami's lead to 31–24. The Canes answered with a drive that stalled at the Nebraska 25-yard line, but

Davis missed a 42-yard field goal attempt that would have sealed the win.

Nebraska then drove deep into Miami territory and was at fourth down and eight from the 24-yard line when Smith took a pitch from Gill and scored to bring the Cornhuskers to within a point with 48 seconds left on the clock. Kicking an extra point would have tied the score. Nebraska, with a 12–0–1 record, would have been named champion, but coach Tom Osborne and his team didn't want to back into the title with a tie, so they elected to go for a two-point conversion to win the game and the championship. But Gill's pass to Smith was tipped away by safety Ken Calhoun, and the University of Miami had its first national championship team.

Schnellenberger Struggles as UM Soars

Howard Schnellenberger left Miami with a 41–16 record and an offer to coach in the USFL, but that opportunity fell through. The man who had started the year as the hottest commodity in college coaching was idle when the 1984 season began that fall. A year later, he took the coaching job at Louisville, a program that rivaled Miami's—in 1978.

Meanwhile, under new coach Jimmy Johnson, UM faltered in 1984 but regained its footing as an elite program in 1985, consistently finishing in the top 10 over the next nine years. Schnellenberger spent 10 years at Louisville, one at Oklahoma and has just finished his 10th at Florida Atlantic, an hour up I-95 from Miami. Whatever magic he possessed at UM deserted him when he left the program. In the 21 seasons since Schnellenberger left the Orange Bowl as the coach of the national champion Hurricanes, he has had a very ordinary 116–122–3 record with just one team that has finished in the top 20.

The Sour Before the Sweet

Hurricane fans looked forward to the 1985 season, especially after watching their team's late-season collapse in 1984. Miami lost its last three games, including two at the Orange Bowl. In a week 11 game against Maryland, the Canes blew a 31–0 halftime lead to finish with a 42–40 loss. Maryland's second-half rally to overcome a 31-point deficit set an NCAA record. That crushing defeat was surpassed a week later courtesy of Doug Flutie's Hail Mary touchdown pass on the last play of the game to give Boston College a 47–45 win.

The home losing streak increased to three when Miami dropped its 1985 opener to Florida, 35–23. Fans, boosters and anyone remotely interested in UM football were on the brink of open rebellion, so it was good for all concerned that coach Jimmy Johnson had a chance to right the ship with three consecutive road games, which he did.

The team that returned to the Orange Bowl to host Cincinnati on October 12 was a more focused and determined unit. The Canes were also riding a three-game *winning* streak as they dominated every facet of the game and dispatched their guests from the Midwest 38–0. Visitors to the Orange Bowl for Miami's last three home games didn't fare much better, as the Canes defense allowed just 17 points in wins over Louisville (45–7), Colorado State (24–3) and Notre Dame (58–7). But the win over Cincinnati had particular significance—it started a NCAA record 58-game home winning streak that lasted until a 38–20 loss to Washington on September 24, 1994.

The Cream of the Crop

The last era of Miami dominance took place from 2000 to 2003, when the Hurricanes went 46–4, including a national title in 2001. NFL teams reaped the fruits of that bumper crop as four Miami players were selected in the first round of the 2001 college draft, followed by five in 2002, four in 2003 and a record six in the opening round on draft day 2004.

Miami supplied an astonishing 19 out of 128 blue-chip players over that span. Some of the more noteworthy number ones who have starred in the pros include wide receiver Reggie Wayne (2001), a four-time Pro Bowler with the Colts; New Orleans tight end Jeremy Shockey (2002), who went to four Pro Bowls for the Giants; and six-time Pro Bowl defensive back Ed Reed (2002) of the Baltimore Ravens. The class of 2003 was led by wide receiver Andre Johnson, a four-time Pro Bowler with the Houston Texans.

And four members of the record-setting 2004 draft contingent had that lofty status justified by their peers by earning Pro Bowl berths. They are defensive back Sean Taylor of the Redskins; tight end Kellen Winslow Jr. of the Browns, who has moved on to the Dolphins;

Jonathan Vilma of the Jets; and nose tackle Vince Wilfork of the Patriots.

Florida State Seminoles
Before Bobby, There was Bill

As hard as it may be to fathom, Division I football did exist at Florida State before Bobby Bowden became head coach of the Seminoles in 1976. Although the teams under Bill Peterson didn't contend for a national championship, it was during his 11-year reign that the program gained national recognition.

The native of Toronto, Ohio, took over as coach in 1960 but struggled his first four seasons, earning a 15–19–6 record. The Seminoles opened the 1964 season with three consecutive shutout wins over the University of Miami, Texas Christian and New Mexico State and were more than ready for number five rated Kentucky when the Wildcats came to Tallahassee on October 11.

After the defense forced Kentucky to punt on the opening possession, the Seminoles took over on their own 48-yard line and marched 52 yards on 11 plays for a 6–0 lead en route to a 48–6 win. The most memorable play of the opening drive, and the game, came on the third down at Kentucky's 46, when quarterback Steve Tensi called the ancient "Statue of Liberty" play and halfback Larry Green circled around the left side of the play for a 14-yard gain.

The win elevated FSU to a number 10 ranking in national polls—the first time in Seminole history that they cracked the top 10. It was the high-water mark of a season that ended with a 36–19 win over Oklahoma in the Gator Bowl.

The 1964 campaign was a special season on both a team and a personal level for the Seminoles. The 9–1–1 record was the best in the 11-year history of the program, and wide receiver Fred Biletnikoff became the first FSU player to earn All-American honors.

The Cradle of Championship Coaches

During Bill Peterson's 11-year tenure as coach, he had a staff of some very talented assistants, including Bobby Bowden, Don James, Joe Gibbs and Bill Parcells, who went on to win championships on both collegiate and professional levels.

Don James coached at FSU from 1959 to 1965. He was the defensive coordinator for Peterson and eventually became the head coach at Kent State and later at Washington, where his Huskies (12–0) won a share of the national championship in 1991. Under James, Washington won the Rose Bowl four times and compiled a record of 153–57–2.

Joe Gibbs coached the offensive line for Peterson in 1967–68. In 1981, Gibbs became coach of the Washington Redskins and led the team to four Super Bowl appearances and three championships before stepping down in 1992.

Bill Parcells was hired for the 1970 season, Peterson's last at FSU, to coach linebackers. He was tabbed for the head job with the New York Giants in 1983, where he won the Super Bowl following the 1986 and 1990 seasons.

A QB's Best Friend

Fred Biletnikoff was one of the first prolific wide receivers in college football. In the 1960s, Division I college football offenses were still mired in the "three yards and a cloud of dust" mentality. Peterson and his staff, which by that time included a young assistant named Bobby Bowden, started experimenting with a wide-open passing game and found they were able to take advantage of their receivers, whose talents had been largely ignored until then.

The Erie, Pennsylvania, native was no speed demon, but his precise route-running skills, deceptive moves and sure hands caused headaches for opposing defensive backs in FSU's 9–1–1 1964 season. This son of Russian immigrants made 57 receptions for 987 yards and 11 touchdowns that year and ended his college career with a career best 13 catches for 192 yards and four touchdowns in a win over Oklahoma in the Gator Bowl.

There was no drop-off when Biletnikoff joined the Oakland Raiders of the American Football League (AFL). Once he broke into the starting lineup, he became a favorite target of quarterback Daryle Lamonica and later Ken Stabler. Biletnikoff had six Pro Bowl seasons and was named Most Valuable Player in Oakland's 32–16 win over Minnesota in Super Bowl XI. Biletnikoff was inducted into the Pro Football Hall of

Fame in 1988 and the College Football Hall of Fame in 1991.

Since 1994, the Fred Biletnikoff Award has been given to the best wide receiver in college football.

Modest Expectations

By his own standards, Bobby Bowden's first year as head coach at Florida State was unimpressive. After all, when he came to Tallahassee, the Birmingham, Alabama, native boasted a 73–27 record and had just led West Virginia to a number 20 ranking and a 13–10 victory over North Carolina in the Peach Bowl.

When Bowden finally stepped down as coach in 2009, he was second on the all-time list of victories with 377, behind only Penn State's Joe Paterno. But to Seminole fans, a 5–6 record in 1976 represented one more victory than the team had had over the last three seasons, in which it had gone 4–29.

Bowden recalled the seemingly impossible predicament of making the Seminoles winners in a more humorous light, "When I was at Alabama, they said, 'Beat Auburn.' When I was at West Virginia, they said, 'Beat Pittsburgh.' When I came to Florida State, they said, 'Beat anybody.'" And he eventually did. Bowden went on to build one of the greatest football programs in college history. The Seminoles eventually won two national championships, and their famous coach left the game after the 2009 season with a 377–129–4 record.

Anybody Becomes Everybody

Nobody was laughing after Bowden's second season in Tallahassee—they were cheering! The Seminoles went 10–2, ending the season ranked 14th—the highest in the school's history—and easily beat Texas Tech 40–17 in the Tangerine Bowl.

Bowden's second year at Florida State would also be remembered because it was FSU's first 10-victory season, the school had its first postseason win since 1964 and seven players were named first- or second-team All-American. It also was the first of the coach's Division I record 33 consecutive winning seasons.

Chief Osceola and Renegade

Many Division I programs have traditions that add to their team's lore, and Florida State is no different. Before every home game, in what is considered an act of homage to the Seminole tribe, a student dressed in authentic traditional attire designed by the tribe portrays the great Seminole leader, Chief Osceola. Riding an appaloosa horse named Renegade, the chief leads the team onto the field and plants a flaming spear at midfield.

The idea of the Chief Osceola and Renegade pregame ritual was conceived by Bill Durham, an FSU student during the 1960s. The idea was repeatedly rejected until Bowden heard about it when he came to Tallahassee. Durham sought and obtained the approval of the Seminole Tribe of Florida to allow the team to portray Osceola, and the ceremony was first introduced for the opening game of the 1978 season against Oklahoma State. Durham and his family supply the horse, and an FSU student portrays the chief, whose indomitable spirit has added to the legacy of one of the best programs in college football.

The Sod Cemetery

On Saturday afternoons each autumn, college football teams and their fans observe rituals as the visiting teams, with at least one exception, look on. When waiting for the opening kickoff for road games in which they're considered underdogs, Seminole players focus on adding to the Sod Cemetery that lies just outside the gates of the practice field on the FSU campus.

When Florida State was preparing to play a road game at Georgia in 1962, one of the school's professors, Dean Coyle Moore, gave a speech to the team and at one point challenged them to "bring back some sod from between the hedges at Georgia." The underdog Seminoles promptly upset the Bulldogs 18–0. Team captain Gene McDowell brought back a piece of sod from the field at Athens and presented it to Moore. It was then buried at the corner of the practice field with a plaque commemorating the win, and the Sod Cemetery was born.

Each piece of sod in the "cemetery" is accompanied by a tombstone that states the game score and the date of the victory. At first, the Seminoles only brought back sod after upset wins on the road. As the football program became more successful, all bowl games were considered "sod games," as were "landmark games," whether the team was the underdog or not. Today there are more than 70 tombstones in the cemetery.

Solid Footwork Brings First National Title

By 1993, Seminole fans had grown accustomed to winning. But now winning wasn't enough. Nor was winning bowl games or finishing not lower than fourth in the postseason rankings for six consecutive years. Many believed the program was on equal footing with the obnoxious Miami Hurricanes, but the Seminoles' intrastate rivals to the south had won four national championships, while FSU had none.

So the Seminoles entered the 1993 season with a monkey, which felt more like a gorilla, on their backs. Once again, they entered a season ranked number one and finished the regular season 11–1, the only blemish coming against Notre Dame. Their opponents in the Orange Bowl that season were the Nebraska Cornhuskers (11–0), who they'd beaten 27–14 in the Miami-based bowl game the previous year.

The Seminole offense, which was led by Heisman Trophy–winning quarterback Charlie Ward, had overwhelmed opponents all year, averaging 43 points per game. But FSU managed just one touchdown against the stingy Cornhusker defense and had to settle for four Scott Bently field goals, the last of which gave them an 18–16 lead with 21 seconds left in the game.

Bowden and his players couldn't believe it when Nebraska quarterback Tommie Frazier completed a 29-yard pass to tight end Trumane Bell that set up a 45-yard field goal attempt with one second left.

FSU had been knocked out of title contention by failed last-second field goal attempts against Miami. Now they were relying on an errant kick to win their first national championship, which they did when Byron Bennett's kick sailed wide left.

Florida's College QBs Usually at Home on Super Sunday

In the history of the Super Bowl, 29 quarterbacks have led their team to the NFL championship, but only one of them played his college ball in the Sunshine State. Florida-based running backs and receivers, however, have fared considerably better on Super Bowl Sunday.

Former Florida State quarterback Brad Johnson capped his best year in the NFL with a workman-like performance in guiding Tampa Bay over Oakland 48–21 in Super Bowl XXXVII. Johnson succeeded where other noteworthy signal callers from the Sunshine State's deep pool of football talent failed. In the Super Bowl era, Florida has produced seven Heisman Trophy winners and eight first-round NFL draft picks. Miami's Jim Kelly and Gator Rex Grossman had their opportunities, with Buffalo and Chicago, respectively, while Bernie Kosar earned a ring as a backup with Dallas in Super Bowl XXVIII.

The backs they handed off to and the receivers who caught their passes have been more successful on pro football's big day. Running back Emmitt Smith didn't win a national championship as a Gator, but he won three Lombardi Trophies with Dallas; former

Hurricane Pete Banaszak scored two touchdowns in Oakland's 32–16 win over Minnesota in Super Bowl XI; West Palm Beach native Ottis Anderson, who starred in the UM backfield in the mid-1970s, ran for 102 yards on 21 carries and was named MVP in the Giants' thrilling 20–19 win over Buffalo in Super Bowl XXV; and Edgar Bennett, who stood next to Johnson in the Seminole huddle in the early 1990s, was a starter in Green Bay's 35–21 win over New England in Super Bowl XXXI.

Like Smith, former Hurricane receiver Michael Irvin won three championships in Dallas. Another Hurricane, Kevin Williams, started opposite Irvin in the Cowboys' 27–17 win over the Steelers in Super Bowl XXX. Reggie Wayne became the third Miami receiver to enjoy a victory party after the big game when the Colts beat the Bears 29–17 in Miami following the 2006 season. In Super Bowl II, Fred Biletnikoff's Raiders got trounced by the Packers, but the former Seminole was on the other end nine years later when he and Raiders teammate Banaszak beat the Vikings. Dennis McKinnon went undrafted when his playing days as a Gator ended, but he spent seven seasons in the NFL, four as a starting receiver and return man for the Chicago Bears, including their championship team of 1985 that beat New England 46–10 in Super Bowl XX.

Chapter Two

Fins, Bucs and Jags

Florida sports fans, like fans around the rest of the country, have been passionate about their football since the turn of the last century. But until the 1970s, residents of the Sunshine State never got to see championship-level football from any of their college teams. Instead, they had to settle for the indignity of watching schools from outside Florida play in the annual Orange Bowl game in Miami. They got another taste of high-caliber football when the AFL and NFL champions squared off in Miami following the 1967, 1968 and 1970 seasons for something called the Super Bowl.

But that all changed in 1970 when Don Shula agreed to coach the Miami Dolphins. Within two years, the Dolphins, who never had a winning season before Shula's arrival, were playing in the Super Bowl, and a year later, they won their first championship. Then, in 1976, Central Florida was awarded an expansion team, the Tampa Bay Buccaneers. After a horrendous start, the Bucs made their first playoff appearance in 1979. In 1995, the Jacksonville Jaguars played their first game, and a year later, they upset Buffalo and Denver before falling to New England in the AFC Championship game.

The Dolphins, Bucs and Jags have had their share of tough seasons recently, but football fans in Florida know they'll get to see at least one of the local college or pro teams win during the weekend.

Miami Dolphins

The Champ Was Right!

Former heavyweight boxing champion Charles "Sonny" Liston lived in Philadelphia in the early 1960s but grew to hate the city and eventually moved west to Colorado. When asked to assess his feelings about the city regarded as the "Cradle of Democracy," he remarked, "I'd rather be a lamppost in Denver than the mayor of Philadelphia."

No one knows for sure if the Dolphins' first owner, Joe Robbie, was aware of Liston's sentiments, but when the Minnesota-based lawyer approached AFL commissioner Joe Foss to inquire about purchasing a franchise in the league, he had his sights set on the City of Brotherly Love. Foss, a good friend of Robbie's from their college days at the University of South Dakota, convinced him to locate his team in South Florida instead.

Unlike Philadelphia, which had the NFL Eagles, there was no professional sports franchise in the Sunshine State. Ever the shrewd businessman, Robbie agreed. He soon had the support of Miami's mayor and secured an agreement to play his home games in the historic Orange Bowl. With television star Danny Thomas as his chief partner, Robbie was able to come up with the $7.5 million franchise fee and was awarded the new AFL team when the league owners met on August 16, 1965.

Robbie let the team's new fans take part in determining its name, and more than 20,000 offered suggestions. The name he finally settled on was the Dolphins.

Robbie Uses Star Power

Robbie's friend and fellow Lebanese American, actor Danny Thomas, was instrumental in helping with financing to purchase the Dolphins. At the time, Thomas was starring in his own hit television series, *Make Room for Daddy*. The actor also brought considerable gravitas to the enterprise; Thomas had founded the internationally renowned St. Jude's Children's Hospital in Nashville, Tennessee.

Robbie was also friends with Vice President Hubert Humphrey, whom he had known since Humphrey was mayor of Minneapolis in the mid-1940s. Once he had the ownership secured, Robbie continued to seek out marquee attractions that would help the Dolphins gain national exposure—and what could be better than cashing in on the world's most famous dolphin, Flipper?

Flipper was a television series that ran on NBC from 1964 to 1967 and centered around a park ranger and his two sons who befriended a dolphin. In 1966, Robbie had a pool installed behind the end zone at the open end of the Orange Bowl, and a dolphin from the local aquarium was transported to the stadium on game days.

Looking to make an impact on the field, Robbie hired former Detroit Lions coach George Wilson to lead the Dolphins. Wilson had mild success with the Lions; his teams were 53–45–6 from 1957 to 1964, including winning the 1957 NFL championship. Prior to coaching, Wilson had been a standout end on the famous Chicago Bears championship teams of the 1940s known in NFL annals as the "Monsters of the Midway."

Starting Out With a Bang

Few expansion teams in sports history can equal the smashing start that the Miami Dolphins had. Opening the 1966 season against the Oakland Raiders on September 2, Joe Auer returned the opening kick 95 yards for a touchdown. Present on the sidelines for the inaugural game was co-owner Danny Thomas, who was so excited that he ran alongside Auer for most of the way—with a cigar in his mouth! There was little else to celebrate that day, though, as the Dolphins lost 23–14.

The team didn't win its first game until week six, a 24–7 win over Denver at the Orange Bowl. Having little success moving the ball on offense, the Dolphins used four different quarterbacks that year. In fact, they were so desperate that their quarterback for their first win had not even played during college. His name? George Wilson Jr., the coach's son.

Robbie Turns the Tables on the Media

The Dolphins' early years were an exercise in frustration for Robbie. Managing the expansion team's finances and trying to build a respectable product on the field was a daunting task. It didn't help matters to have a cynical media analyzing your every move.

A man who didn't suffer fools gladly, Robbie decided to see if the local South Florida media could handle the scrutiny when the roles were reversed. The owner devoted a portion of the game programs that were sold at the Orange Bowl for home games to monitoring the media's performance.

He interviewed local sports editors and asked them the same types of questions that he had to answer. After all, Robbie said, it's the public's right to know. How much did the staff get paid? What was the total budget for the sports department compared to other newspapers? Why didn't they send photographers to Dolphins away games? Could it be because they were cheapskates? When mistakes appeared in the paper, was it because the writers and editors were incompetent or did they simply not care? The owner also inquired about salacious gossip overheard in the newsroom. When Robbie was asked if he planned to print an item without checking its veracity, he answered that he wouldn't, but the gossip columnist he had hired probably would.

The embattled owner made his point—the press should be held to the same standards to which it held the people and institutions it covered.

Laying the Foundation

Although Miami never had a winning season under head coach George Wilson, Dolphins fans do owe him a bit of gratitude. Wilson drafted some of the players who would eventually blossom and become key components on Don Shula's squads, which went on to play in three consecutive Super Bowls.

The only significant contributor in Wilson's initial draft class came in round 12 with the selection of wide receiver Howard Twilley. The Tulsa, Oklahoma, standout played 11 seasons in South Florida and had the honor of catching the team's first touchdown pass in Super Bowl VII against Washington.

Coming off a pitiful 3–11 first season, the Dolphins' top priority in 1967 was finding a quarterback. Wilson struck gold with the fourth-overall pick in the first round that year, taking Purdue star quarterback Bob Griese. Tight end and punter Larry Seiple of Kentucky never made All-Pro, but the seventh-round pick's deceptive qualities and quick feet came in handy during the 1972 playoffs, helping to keep the perfect season alive.

Wilson tabbed three future Pro Bowlers in 1968. Bruising fullback Larry Csonka was selected in the first round (eighth overall), safety Dick Anderson in the third and running back Jim Kiick in round five.

For what would be his final draft in 1969, Wilson selected defensive linemen Bill Stanfill of Georgia and Bob Heinz of Pacific in the first two rounds, respectively, and went back to offense in round three, taking running back Mercury Morris of West Texas A&M.

Wilson's Two Major Moves Eventually Help Miami

Coach Wilson made two key decisions that paid huge dividends for the Dolphins, but the decisions were made while he was still at the helm of the Detroit Lions. In 1957, Wilson had grown tired of the antics of legendary quarterback Bobby Layne, who had a reputation as both a hard drinker and a hard player.

Wilson was convinced that Layne's lifestyle was responsible for the quarterback missing the second half of Detroit's 1957 championship season. Figuring that he had won an NFL championship without Layne, Wilson traded the popular future Hall of Famer to Pittsburgh for a then-24-year-old, unaccomplished signal caller named Earl Morrall.

In 1960, Wilson added a young defensive assistant, Don Shula, from the University of Kentucky, to his staff. While in Detroit, Shula got to observe Morrall. By 1968, Shula was the head coach at Baltimore and traded for Morrall to back up Johnny Unitas. When Unitas was injured, Morrall stepped in and guided the Colts to a 13–1 record. Unfortunately, Shula and Morrall had to live with the ignominy of losing Super Bowl III to the Jets.

Morrall would finally deliver for Shula in 1972. As coach of the Dolphins, Shula obtained Morrall again, this time to back up Bob Griese. When Griese went down in week five with a broken leg, Morrall stepped in and guided the Dolphins to nine consecutive wins as Miami finished the season 14–0. He added another win in the divisional round of the playoffs before stepping aside for Griese in the AFC championship game.

Two weeks later, the Dolphins beat Washington 14–7 in Super Bowl VII to complete their perfect season.

Adios, Flipper!

After three seasons, the series *Flipper* was dropped from NBC's 1968 fall schedule. By their third season, Robbie and Wilson had acquired a few land-based Dolphins such as quarterback Bob Griese and running backs Larry Csonka and Jim Kiick, who appeared to have brighter futures than the former TV star. Unable to reach an agreement with the city of Miami on who should pay for Flipper the dolphin's Sunday afternoons at the Orange Bowl, Robbie placed the aquatic mascot on irrevocable waivers.

The Long Road to Canton

Hard work, intelligence, discipline and determination were the hallmarks of Don Shula's coaching style. These were qualities that served him well during his career as a football player and coach. Although they're an important part of any successful person's character, they also help you get noticed.

In 1947, the summer after he graduated from high school, Shula's decision to fill up his near-empty gas tank led to a chance meeting with a former opponent that changed his life forever. At five feet, 11 inches tall and weighing less than 200 pounds, Shula didn't receive any scholarship offers, despite being an All-State quarterback in his senior high school season.

Shula was born and raised in Grand River, Ohio, a small town on Lake Erie not far from the Pennsylvania border. The western Pennsylvania–Ohio region is also a deep reservoir of football talent. But it was Shula's misfortune that the field of potential college football stars was overly crowded because of the abundance of veterans who had returned from World War II.

Assessing the situation, Shula decided to get a job and work for a year so he could afford to pay for college. Playing football was a distant dream. So was working in the family business. Shula's father, Dan, was a commercial fisherman on Lake Erie, but the young Shula's inability to stomach rough seas convinced him that his life's path, wherever it took him, would be on land.

At the gas station that fateful summer, he bumped into a man named Howard Bachman, a coach at one of the local high schools who had seen Shula play. Bachman asked the youngster what his future plans were. When Shula replied that he was planning to get a job, Bachman advised him not to and suggested an alternative.

Bachman was friends with the new coach at John Carroll University, which was located between Grand River and Cleveland and less than an hour's drive from Shula's home. Bachman said he would set up an interview for the young man. After meeting with coach Herb Eisele, Shula was offered a partial scholarship for his freshman year. He was also told that the scholarship could be upgraded to a full ride if his performance merited it. Based on an impressive first season, Shula got the full scholarship.

Decisions, Decisions...

After graduating from college in 1951, Shula, who had majored in sociology and minored in math, was offered a job teaching math and coaching football at a high school in Canton, Ohio. The teaching job paid $3250 per year. But any recognition for his contribution and success as a football coach in Canton would have to wait, because Shula was selected by the Cleveland Browns in the seventh round of the 1951 NFL draft. The Browns offered him a contract for $5000.

It turns out that Shula's coach at John Carroll, Herb Eisele, was a devotee of Paul Brown, the innovative coach of the Cleveland Browns. Eisele attended many of Brown's coaching clinics and modeled his approach to the game after Brown's, right down to the terminology used in the playbook.

Paul Brown knew Eisele, so he knew that in Shula, he was getting a player who could easily adapt to the demanding Cleveland system. After two seasons with the Browns, Shula was traded to the Baltimore Colts and coach Weeb Ewbank. Shula played four seasons in Baltimore before closing out his career as a player in 1957 with the Washington Redskins. He ended his playing career with 21 interceptions and four fumble recoveries.

Leaving His Mark on the Game

As a player, Shula was known for his hard work and intelligence, but he never impressed the sportswriters enough to be named All-Pro, nor his contemporaries enough to be voted to the Pro Bowl. Yet he did have the respect of his teammates and coaches on the Baltimore Colts, who named him a team captain on defense. In 1955, he helped mentor a young rookie receiver out of Southern Methodist University named Raymond Berry.

Selected in the 20th round of the NFL draft, Berry had little hope of making the team, let alone the Hall of Fame. Years later, he reminisced that those first two years in the NFL were the toughest of his life, and he was always grateful for the tutoring and mentoring he received from the veteran Shula, against whom he practiced every day.

Although they were teammates for just two seasons, Shula had an even bigger impact on Berry's career after Shula was cut by the Colts following the 1956 season. He was then signed by the Washington Redskins in 1957 for what would be his seventh and final season as a player.

Against the Redskins on November 10, Berry would be defended against, if you can call it that, by his old mentor. Teaming up with new starting quarterback Johnny Unitas, the future six-time Pro Bowler and Hall of Famer burned Shula and anyone else the Redskins put on him for a club record 12 catches, 237 yards and two touchdowns. Berry ended the season leading the Colts receivers in catches and yards gained.

Six years later, Berry was once again under Shula's direction when his former teammate became head coach of the Colts. Berry retired after the 1967 season as Baltimore's career leader in receptions, yards and touchdowns.

In 1985, Berry figured prominently in yet another chapter in Shula's life, this time as head coach of the New England Patriots. The teams split their regular season meetings, with each team winning at home. In the AFC Championship game, played at the Orange Bowl, Berry's squad took advantage of six Miami turnovers and cruised to a 31–14 win, advancing to Super Bowl XX in New Orleans against the Chicago Bears.

Keep Your Friends Close and Your Enemies Closer

Many of the coaches Shula played for or against had a prominent role in his career even after they parted ways. He ended up replacing his former boss, Weeb Ewbank, as the head coach of the Baltimore Colts when Ewbank took the head coaching job with the New York Jets of the AFL in 1963. Their teams eventually squared off in one of the most important games in pro football history, Super Bowl III.

After coaching defensive backs at the University of Virginia in 1958, Shula joined his old position coach with the Browns, Blanton Collier, who had replaced Bear Bryant as the head man at the University of Kentucky. It's worth noting that like Shula, Ewbank and Collier were also coaching disciples of Paul Brown.

After a year with the Wildcats, Shula entered the pro ranks in 1960 for a three-year stint with the Detroit Lions. His boss with the Lions was George Wilson, who, in 1966, would be named the first coach of the new AFL expansion team in Miami. After four losing seasons, Shula replaced Wilson in Miami.

A Good Quarterback Equals Good Luck

Building a championship team is a formidable task. A coach needs good assistants, great players and a little bit of luck. Shula once said, "Luck means a lot in football. Not having a good quarterback is bad luck."

Consider that Paul Brown had Otto Graham, Vince Lombardi had Bart Starr, Tom Landry had Roger Staubach, Chuck Noll had Terry Bradshaw and Bill Walsh had Joe Montana. A few coaches were fortunate enough to cultivate the careers of more than one great signal caller. Weeb Ewbank had Johnny Unitas and Joe Namath, and Joe Gibbs won Super Bowls with Joe Theismann, Doug Williams and Mark Rypien. Shula won championships with Unitas, Earl Morrall and Bob Griese, and went to Super Bowls with David Woodley and Dan Marino. For Shula, luck, as the old saying goes, was the residue of design.

A Very Merry Win

In 1971, Miami won its first AFC East division title with a 10–3–1 record and advanced to the playoffs for the second consecutive year. But, having lost to Oakland in a first-round playoff game in 1970, the team was still looking for its first postseason win. They say you never forget your first love. Well, the Dolphins and their fans will never forget the team's first playoff win.

The Dolphins traveled to Kansas City to face the Chiefs on Christmas Day. Coached by Hank Stram, the Chiefs still had many of their veterans who had played in Super Bowls I and IV. With future Hall of Fame quarterback Len Dawson leading the offense,

Kansas City took an early 10-point lead. Miami, with its powerful ground game, proved it wasn't a one-dimensional offense. The Chiefs defense, which ranked third against the run, plugged the running lanes on Csonka and Kiick, so Griese took to the air to take advantage of receiver Paul Warfield's skills.

Csonka's one-yard touchdown run cut the deficit to 10–7. Then, with less than a minute to play in the second quarter, Chiefs running back Ed Podolak, who was in the midst of a career day, made a costly fumble that safety Dick Anderson recovered on the Kansas City seven-yard line. Yepremian's 14-yard field goal tied the score at 10 as the first half ended.

The teams traded one-yard touchdown runs in the third quarter and entered the final quarter of regulation time tied at 17. Dawson's 65-yard pass to Elmo Wright set up Podolak's three-yard touchdown run, putting the Chiefs ahead 24–17 with just under seven minutes left in the game.

On the ensuing possession, Griese marched the Dolphins down the field, with Warfield making two clutch receptions. Griese then hit tight end Marv Fleming from the five-yard line for a touchdown with 1:37 left, and Yepremian added the extra point to tie the score at 24.

The game was far from over as Podolak fielded the kickoff at the goal line and returned it 78 yards to the Miami 22. Three running plays later, Jan Stenerud, who had missed a 30-yard field goal attempt in the second quarter, was called on to attempt the game-winning kick with 35 seconds left. But the future Hall of Fame kicker missed, with the ball going wide right, and the NFL had its first overtime playoff game since the Colts vs. Giants epic of 1958.

The Chiefs won the coin toss and elected to receive. Miami tried to keep the ball out of Podolak's hands on the kickoff, but a Kansas City lineman lateralled to the all-purpose back, who returned it to the 46. Dawson then threw two passes to Podolak, who moved the ball into Miami territory. The drive stalled on the 35-yard line, and Stenerud was once again called upon to end the game. But Nick Buoniconti broke through and blocked the 42-yard field goal attempt to give the Dolphins life.

Later in the overtime period, Miami crossed the midfield, but Yepremian's 52-yard field goal attempt fell short, and the first overtime quarter ended without a score. On the second possession of what was now the longest game in pro football history, Griese handed off to Csonka, who had been muzzled so far by the Chiefs defense. But the bruising fullback broke through and rambled 29 yards to the Kansas City 36-yard line. Then Miami advanced the ball to the 30. This time, Yepremian split the uprights from 37 yards to give Miami its first playoff win in a game that took 82 minutes and 42 seconds.

It was a game for the ages. It catapulted Miami into the NFL elite and was also the last playoff appearance for one of the great Kansas City teams coached by Hank Stram. Podolak was the star in a losing effort. He gained 350 all-purpose yards and scored two of Kansas City's three touchdowns. Nearly 40 years later, it remains the longest game in NFL history.

Pre–Super Bowl Shocker

A few days before Super Bowl VI in New Orleans, some Dolphins players went out for a night on the town and hit one of the clubs along Bourbon Street, looking to have a couple of drinks and test their luck with the local females. The players were soon chatting with a group of voluptuous patrons. The Dolphins players' hopes of taking home these brief acquaintances was doused when someone realized that the targets of their attention weren't women, but were, in fact, female impersonators hired by the club. The players were furious and tore the place up. The police had to be called in to restore calm. Bourbon Street wasn't the only place the Dolphins had problems scoring that week. On Super Sunday, the Miami offense was shut down in a 24–3 loss to Dallas.

Not a "One-Year" Wonder

The Miami Dolphins of the early 1970s made a then-unprecedented three consecutive trips to the Super Bowl. To say that they did it their own way is an understatement. Shula's teams dominated both sides of the ball on a level that ranks in the upper echelon of any of pro football's dynasties.

At a time when pro football was becoming a pass-happy game, the Dolphins actually ran for more yards than they passed—sometimes by as much as 1000 yards—during those seasons. Yet the offense ranked fourth, first and third, respectively, in points scored during the team's Super Bowl run in 1971, 1972 and 1973. The only other Super Bowl champions to win with a ground game that outpaced its air attack were the Pittsburgh Steelers of 1973 and 1974.

Consider that Griese, Csonka, Paul Warfield, Larry Little and Jim Langer are in the Hall of Fame, and Morrall, running back Mercury Morris, guard Bob Kuechenberg and tackles Norm Evans and Wayne Moore earned trips to the Pro Bowl during that era. Tight end Marv Fleming and receivers Howard Twilley and Marlin Briscoe were the only starters not to earn All-Pro status.

Defensive coordinator Bill Arnsparger was the architect of the famed "No Name" defense that caused havoc for the rest of the NFL. Miami's defense ranked seventh out of 11 AFL teams in 1969, its last year under head coach Wilson. With the addition of players such as linebacker Nick Buoniconti, who was obtained in a trade with the Patriots, the Dolphins quickly became one of the top defensive units, finishing the 1970 season ranked fifth in points allowed in the 24-team NFL.

The Dolphins defense improved to third in 1971, and the team was the statistical and acknowledged best of the NFL in its two championship seasons that followed. Even so, only four players, Buoniconti, defensive end Bill Stanfill and safeties Dick Anderson and Jake Scott, made the Pro Bowl.

The Greatest Running Attack in NFL History

To say that the Miami ground game was nonpareil in pro football history is not a matter of opinion. The team's offense cruised to five consecutive trips to the playoffs behind the three-headed monster of

Larry Csonka, Jim Kiick and Mercury Morris. The Dolphins were 57–12 against regular season opponents from 1970 to 1974.

During their two championship seasons, Miami steamrolled their opposition in the playoffs as well. Consider that against the NFL's best defenses, Miami completed only 24 of 40 passes for 297 yards in defeating Cleveland and Pittsburgh in the 1972 playoffs and then Washington in Super Bowl VII. In those games, the Dolphins' ground attack totaled 575 yards on 131 carries.

In the 1973 playoffs and the Super Bowl, Miami passers completed a total of 20 of 31 passes for 266 yards. Even though Cincinnati, Oakland and Minnesota's famed "Purple People Eaters" knew the Dolphins were going to run, they still couldn't stop them. The result—Miami gained 703 yards on 158 carries.

Raiders and Injuries End a Dynasty

Like all sports dynasties, world-class talent mixed with some good fortune is the key to sustaining a multi-championship run. Such was the case for the Dolphins of the early 1970s. The team was so talented that it was able to overcome the loss of starting quarterback Bob Griese midway through its first championship season.

The 1974 Dolphins won their fourth consecutive AFC East title with an 11–3 record and headed to Oakland to take on the AFC West champion Raiders, coached by John Madden and led by quarterback Ken Stabler. The December 21 contest at the Oakland

Coliseum is remembered as one of the most hotly contested playoff games in NFL history, with the lead changing hands seven times.

Miami's goal was to score first with its time-consuming running attack, thus controlling the tempo of the game. However, nobody expected the Dolphins to grab a 7–0 lead when rookie return man Nat Moore returned the opening kickoff for a touchdown. Oakland tied the score early in the second quarter when Stabler connected with Charlie Smith on a 31-yard touchdown pass. The Dolphins went into halftime with a 10–7 lead courtesy of a Garo Yepremian 33-yard field goal. But coach Shula was concerned because he lost the services of two starters, safety Dick Anderson and cornerback Curtis Johnson, who went down with injuries and were unable to play in the second half.

Oakland took advantage of Miami's backups in the secondary as Stabler took to the air with a pair of touchdown passes, a 13-yarder to Fred Biletnikoff and a 72-yard play to Cliff Branch, giving the Raiders a 21–19 lead midway through the fourth quarter. With its championship reign in peril, the Dolphins responded as great champions do—Griese led his team on a drive that culminated with Benny Malone's 23-yard touchdown run with 2:01 remaining in the game.

Stabler, who finished the game completing 20 of 30 passes for 293 yards and four touchdowns, responded with a picture-perfect drive. The former Alabama star completed all six of his passes, the last of which he threw as he was being tackled by Miami defensive end Vern Den Herder. But the Dolphins lineman was a second too late, and Stabler got off a desperation pass to Clarence Davis, who was smothered by Miami defenders in the end zone. But Davis hung on for the touchdown to give Oakland a 26–24 win with 21 seconds remaining.

Miami Had the Oranges, But Buffalo Had "The Juice"

O.J., that is. Shula's championship Miami teams of the early 1970s had arguably the greatest ground attack in NFL history. Larry Csonka, Jim Kiick and Mercury Morris all made the Pro Bowl at least twice, and the Dolphins never finished lower than fourth running the ball during Shula's first five years at the helm.

While the most formidable ground attack called the Orange Bowl home, the best and most exciting back in pro football played his home games in Buffalo. Shula used a three-pronged attack, while the lowly Buffalo Bills relied on 1968 Heisman Trophy–winner O.J. Simpson from the University of Southern California. Shula's "No Name" defense had some success in keeping the four-time NFL rushing champion in check, holding him under 90 yards in their first eight head-to-head contests.

In their second meeting of the 1973 season, Simpson rushed for 120 yards on 20 carries in a game that the Dolphins won 17–0. Simpson ended the season, which at the time was 14 games, with a league-record 2003 yards, but the Dolphins finished by repeating as Super Bowl champs.

Simpson ran against the vaunted Miami "No Name" defense 16 times during his career with Buffalo and gained a very respectable 1117 yards on 240 carries for a 4.9 average. However, Shula would be quick to point out that despite the future Hall of Famer's success, Miami won all 16 games.

Great Play, Great Game, Bad Outcome

The Dolphins finished the 1981 season 11–4–1, which was good enough to host the San Diego Chargers in a first-round playoff game at the Orange Bowl. Miami boasted one of the best defenses in the league that year, which would be challenged by San Diego quarterback Dan Fouts, who led the NFL's top-scoring offense and the number one rated passing attack.

Although second-year quarterback David Woodley struggled at times, coach Shula was fortunate to have Don Strock, who made several appearances in relief. This two-pronged approach, supplemented by the running of Tony Nathan and Andra Franklin, made the offense respectable, but hardly comparable to their opponents on that day.

San Diego dominated the first quarter, jumping out to a 24–0 lead. Miami fans were numb, but Shula remained focused, replacing an ineffective Woodley with Strock. The momentum changed in the second quarter as the Miami defense found its footing, and Strock led the Dolphins on two drives that produced 10 points.

After San Diego missed a 55-yard field goal attempt with 31 seconds remaining in the half, Miami got the ball back on its own 37-yard line. Strock completed two passes to Tom Vigorito, which moved the ball to the 48-yard line, and another to Nathan, who was stopped at the San Diego 40-yard line with six seconds left.

Miami called a timeout, everyone thought, to decide on whether or not to try a quick pass to give kicker Uwe von Schamann a better chance at a field goal or to throw a Hail Mary pass into the end zone. No one at the Orange Bowl, or the millions watching on television, was expecting the play that Shula gave to Strock.

On what turned out to be one of the most memorable plays in NFL history, Strock threw to receiver Durriel Harris, who caught the ball near the right hash mark at the 25. Just as Harris was about to be tackled, he pitched the ball to Nathan at the 29, who sprinted to the end zone for the touchdown as time expired. The play, known as the "Hook and Ladder," reduced what had been a 24-point deficit just 15 minutes earlier to a mere seven.

Miami tied the score early in the third quarter when tight end Joe Rose caught a 15-yard touchdown pass from Strock. Then San Diego answered with a six-play, 60-yard drive capped by a 25-yard touchdown pass from Fouts to Kellen Winlsow to retake the lead.

If anyone doubted that this game was taking on epic proportions, those doubts were relieved when Miami answered with a six-play—all passes—touchdown drive of its own. Strock's 50-yard pass to tight end Bruce Hardy followed by the extra point tied the score at 31.

Nathan's 12-yard touchdown run on the opening play of the fourth quarter and von Schamann's extra point gave Miami a 38–31 lead. The Dolphins held the lead for the next 10 minutes and drove to within field goal range, when Andra Franklin fumbled and the Chargers recovered on their own 18. What should have been a very makeable von Schamann field goal and a 10-point lead for Miami turned into a game-tying drive for San Diego as Fouts hit Brooks with a nine-yard touchdown pass with just under a minute left to play in regulation. Rolf Benirschke's extra point tied the score at 38.

There was enough time left for Miami to win, and Strock drove the Dolphins to the Chargers 26-yard line. But von Schamann's 43-yard field goal attempt was blocked by Winslow to send the game into overtime.

The extra quarter would prove no less dramatic as both teams blew chances to end the game on their first possessions. San Diego won the coin toss and elected to receive. Once again, Fouts drove the Chargers to within field goal range, but a bad snap caused Benirschke to miss from 27 yards. Miami answered with a drive of their own deep into San Diego territory, but once again, a San Diego defender blocked von Schamann's field goal attempt, this time from 34 yards.

Taking over on their own 10-yard line, Fouts directed an 80-yard drive that left Benirschke with another chance to end the game from 29 yards. This time he split the uprights to give the Chargers a 41–38 win with 1:08 left in the fifth quarter.

It was a tough game to lose and a heartbreaking way for Miami to end the season, but it could have been worse. San Diego had to play the AFC Championship game against the Bengals the following week in frigid Cincinnati. Battling subzero temperatures as well as the hometown Bengals, the Chargers lost 27–7.

No 1000-yard Rushers for Shula's Last 17 Years

Throughout his career as a coach, Shula was a master of adapting his offensive scheme to fit his personnel. With the Colts, he let Unitas be Unitas, and in his early years with the Dolphins, he went to three consecutive Super Bowls with arguably the most potent running attack in NFL history.

He continued to win as those championship teams aged or retired throughout the 1970s and early '80s, and then switched to a lethal air attack with the arrival of Dan Marino in 1983. The Dolphins continued to win, but it's worth noting that from 1979 to 1995, no Miami running back broke the 1000-yard barrier, yet the Dolphins made two more trips to the Super Bowl, made the playoffs eight times and had just one losing season.

Delvin Williams, who ran for 1258 yards in 1978, was the last Dolphins runner to pass the 1000-yard mark until Karim Abdul-Jabbar did it in 1996 when he gained 1116 yards under new coach Jimmy Johnson. During that span, only one other team, the Green Bay Packers, failed to have a 1000-yard runner.

The Killer B's

The "No Names" of the 1970s gave way to the "Killer B's" in the early 1980s: left defensive end Doug Betters, nose tackle Bob Baumhower, right end Kim Bokamper, linebackers Bob Brudzinski and Charles Bowser, and the Blackwood brothers, Glenn and Lyle, at free safety and strong safety, respectively. The unit anchored a defense that ranked among the NFL's elite as Miami made the playoffs every year from 1981 to 1985, including two Super Bowl appearances, in 1983 and 1985.

Baumhower, who graduated from Palm Beach Gardens High School and played under Bear Bryant at Alabama, made the Pro Bowl five times. Betters and Bokamper also had Pro Bowl seasons during their careers in Miami. The rest of the Killer Bs defense consisted of linebackers A.J. Duhe, Larry Gordon and Earnest Rhone, and cornerbacks Don McNeal and Gerald Small.

Marino Finds His Marks

Most Hall of Fame quarterbacks had a great receiver who was their favorite target. And a few signal callers were lucky enough to have two receivers who struck fear into the hearts of NFL defensive backs. Joe Namath had Don Maynard and George Sauer, Ken Stabler had Cliff Branch and Fred Biletnikoff, and Terry Bradshaw had Lynn Swann and John Stallworth. Dan Marino and his two favorite targets, the Marks—Clayton and Duper—certainly belong on that list of noteworthy trios.

Although Duper arrived in Miami a year before Marino and Clayton, all made their first big splash in week six during the 1983 season. Miami was 3–2 after five games, but the offense was sputtering under quarterback David Woodley. The Dolphins had scored a total of just 35 points in their last three games.

The fans present at the Orange Bowl that day saw a glimpse of the future, as Marino, making his first start, completed 20 of 30 passes for 322 yards and three touchdowns in a 38–35 loss to Buffalo. Duper had seven catches for 202 yards, and Clayton added two receptions and a touchdown as well.

Marino started nine games and finished the year with 20 touchdown passes—an unspectacular number, but the most by any Miami quarterback since 1977. Duper and his new quarterback made the Pro Bowl that year. The Marino era had arrived.

The Pro Bowl duo became a trio in 1984 as Marino set NFL records for completions, yards and touchdown passes. Clayton made 73 catches for 1389 yards (19.0 average) with a then-record 18 touchdown receptions. Duper hauled in 71 receptions for 1306 yards (18.4 average) and eight touchdowns as Miami led the league in scoring and went to the Super Bowl with a 14–2 record.

At a time when professional football players were becoming bigger, stronger and faster, Marino's two favorite targets both stood just five feet, nine inches tall and weighed 180 pounds. Clayton, a 1983 eighth-round draft pick out of Louisville, finished his career with 582 receptions for 8643 yards (15.4 average) with

85 touchdowns and five trips to the Pro Bowl over 11 seasons. Duper, a second-round selection from Northwestern State University in Louisiana, played in three Pro Bowls and caught 511 passes for 8869 yards (17.4 average) with 59 touchdowns.

Chicago's Super Bowl Stumble

Possibly the most obnoxious collection of players assembled on one team in Miami's Super Bowl era was the 1985 Bears. These were the Bears of Jim McMahon, William "The Refrigerator" Perry, head coach Mike Ditka and defensive coordinator Buddy Ryan. Powered by a ferocious defense, Chicago had steamrolled opponents during the 1985 season and came to the Orange Bowl on December 2 sporting a 12-0 record for a showdown with the Dolphins in a nationally televised *Monday Night Football* game.

The contest matched Miami's number two ranked passing attack against the NFL's best defense, which had not allowed a touchdown in more than three games and featured seven starters who either made All-Pro or got voted to the Pro Bowl that season. With many members of the 1972 team in attendance, Marino picked apart the Chicago defense for three touchdowns, and Miami converted a blocked punt late in the second quarter to lead 31-10 at halftime. The Bears never seriously threatened in the second half, and Marino finished with 270 yards passing and three touchdowns as the Dolphins won 38-24.

To appreciate what the Dolphins accomplished that night, consider that during a 55-game span from early in the 1984 season to the midway point of 1987, the Bears allowed more than 29 points in a game just twice.

A Model of Consistency and Success

When Don Shula left the Dolphins following a 9–7 season in 1995, it brought to an end a 33-year coaching career that saw just two losing seasons. He won an NFL championship in 1968 with the Colts, and he then turned a humiliating loss to the Jets in Super Bowl III into a footnote in his legacy by coaching the only undefeated championship team in league history. He guided the Dolphins to five Super Bowl appearances and won the big game twice, following the 1972 and 1973 seasons.

Shula's record of 328 regular season wins seems safe for a very long time. New England's Bill Belichick, who has the most wins of any active coach (162), turns 59 in 2011. Shula's coaching record stands at 328–156–6 and was 19–17 in the postseason, with a record six Super Bowl appearances.

From Bo to Bowwow

In 1978, Bo Derek starred in the movie *10*, in which she portrayed actor Dudley Moore's idea of what the perfect woman should look like. In the history of the Dolphins, the 1972 team was Bo Derek and the 2007 squad was, well, Courtney Love after a weekend bender. Under coach Cam Cameron, the 2007 Dolphins were perfect in their first 13 games—they lost every one of them. They were ranked at or near the bottom of every statistical category.

It was thought that their next opponent, the Baltimore Ravens, was the last realistic chance the Dolphins had of avoiding the NFL's first winless season since the 1976 Buccaneers. The Ravens' record stood at 4–9 when the team came to Miami on December 16, and they were on their way to a 5–11 season. If the Dolphins couldn't beat Baltimore, a 0–16 record looked extremely likely, with the undefeated New England Patriots and a decent Cincinnati Bengals team on deck.

To make matters worse, the Miami franchise was honoring the 1972 Super Bowl champions during halftime of the Ravens game. On a day that saw few highlights, the Dolphins took their first lead of the day, 16–13, with 1:56 left courtesy of a 29-yard field goal by kicker Jay Feely. But Baltimore then drove to the Miami one-yard line and tied the score with eight seconds left to force overtime.

The Ravens offense got the ball first and drove to the Miami 27-yard line, but this time, kicker Matt Stover missed from 44 yards. Two obscure Miami players then stepped into history on the Dolphins' next possession. On a third-down play from the Baltimore 36-yard line, quarterback Cleo Lemon hit receiver Greg Camarillo near midfield.

Camarillo, an undrafted free agent out of Stanford who spent part of the 2006 season with San Diego, had not scored a touchdown since high school. Lemon was a 2005 free agent out of Arkansas State. Camarillo had two steps on the nearest defender when he caught the ball, then sprinted untouched the rest of the way to the end zone and scored what turned out to be the

Dolphins' longest—and most important—play from scrimmage that season, and the 2007 team avoided the record books with a 22–16 win.

The Strange Adventure of Ricky Williams

When Ricky Williams broke Tony Dorsett's 22-year-old NCAA Division I all-time rushing record while playing for the Texas Longhorns, he immediately became one of the top prospects for selection in the 1999 NFL draft. His natural talents on the field were evident, and the New Orleans Saints wanted to get their hands on him so badly that they traded away all of their 1999 draft picks and their first and third picks in 2000 just to select him fifth overall.

A few days later, Saints head coach Mike Ditka and Williams appeared on the cover of ESPN's *The Magazine* dressed as a bride and groom with the title "For Better or Worse." No team had ever had just one selection at an NFL draft, but the Saints believed heavily in what Williams could bring to their team and were willing to gamble. Well, it turned out to be for the worst. The Saints finished the 1999 season with a record of 3–13, and Ditka was promptly fired. After the Saints again failed to make the playoffs in both 2000 and 2001, management decided to trade Williams while he still held value and to get some of the draft picks they had burned through to get him.

The Dolphins were one of the first teams on the phone when Williams became available. They paid a heavy price for the young running back, sending four draft picks to New Orleans, including two first-round choices, so the Dolphins expected great things from the San Diego, California, native. They got what they paid for when Williams finished the 2002 season as the NFL's leading rusher with 1853 yards.

Naturally, Williams' talents on the field made him a hit with Dolphins fans, but it was a different story with the players and the media. During practices and team events, Williams often kept to himself, and in media scrums after games, it was common for him to leave his helmet on during interviews.

"Ricky's just a different guy," former Saints receiver and teammate Joe Horn explained. "People he wanted to deal with, he did. And people he wanted to have nothing to do with, he didn't. No one could understand that. I don't think guys in the locker room could grasp that he wanted to be to himself—you know, quiet. If you didn't understand him and didn't know what he was about, it always kept people in suspense."

The fans were willing to forgive a few eccentricities in return for a star player on the field, but problems kept cropping up for Williams. In December 2003, he tested positive for marijuana and was given a $650,000 fine along with a four-game suspension. Then came the bizarre announcement in July 2004 just before training camp was set to begin, when Williams declared his intention to retire from professional football. Most people did not believe that he would really leave the sport and thought it was just another one of his strange moments that would pass, but on August 2, 2004, Williams made it official and left the Dolphins.

While the Dolphins struggled through a 4–12 season, Williams attended the California College of Ayurveda to study the ancient system of holistic medicine.

Fans were less than pleased with the former running back. Those that had bought his jersey and once cheered him on now taped over his name in protest. Although the Dolphins lacked the elements of a championship team, fans blamed Williams for their team's poor performance. The media attention around the Dolphins and Williams had become a distraction, and most fans were not very forgiving. But when questioned about that time, Williams has always maintained that it was the most "positive thing I've done in my life," allowing him time to find himself.

Yet even after such a horrible season, the Dolphins management was willing to forgive and forget. In July 2005, Williams held a press conference to announce his return to the Miami lineup and express his apologies to the fans for deserting the team. He had a good season, posting six touchdowns and 743 yards, but the Dolphins lost seven of their first 10 games. Miami rallied in late November and December to finish 9–7, but they failed to make the playoffs.

A few days after the end of the season and the Super Bowl, the league announced that Williams had once again tested positive for a banned substance. His previous positive tests had been for marijuana, but this time around, the league did not release any specifics as to what he was taking. However, many believed that the latest test apparently involved a substance other than marijuana and may have been related to his interest in holistic medicine. With no team to call his own, Williams made the odd decision to join the Canadian Football League for the start of its 2006 season. He signed on with the Toronto Argonauts only after agreeing with the Dolphins that he would return to the team in 2007. In an interview with the Canadian newspaper the *Toronto Sun*, Williams gave his reasons for electing to sign with the CFL club.

"I'm not going to say why I am here right now because I don't know," he began. "I can't even tell you that I made the choice to be here. I know it's hard for people to understand what that means, but the way I live my life is that I'm trying to eradicate likes and dislikes. Likes and dislikes are what lead to confusion, anger, discontentment, and I think when you can learn to accept whatever life gives you, then that's the only chance you really have to be truly happy in this life. When I was suspended by the NFL [for the entire 2006 season for a fourth substance-abuse violation], I went to see what was next for me. I was planning to volunteer and teach yoga for the next year, and then I was approached by the Argonauts to come and play football. I looked at the situation and I tried to make the best choice of what life is telling me to do."

Ricky Williams made his Canadian football debut on June 17, 2006, rushing for 97 yards. But just one month later, he suffered a broken arm during a game and was forced to undergo surgery the following day. Shortly after his return, Williams suffered yet another setback when he tore his Achilles tendon. At the end of the season, CFL commissioner Tom Wright, who had never been happy about the arrival of Williams, instated a new rule that would ban any players who had been suspended from the NFL from joining the CFL. Wright decided that Williams had been a distraction during the season and reasoned that if a player had been suspended for an entire season from a league, then that player should not get a free pass to join another. The newspapers dubbed the decision the "Ricky Williams Rule."

In 2007, the love-hate relationship with the Dolphins continued when Williams returned to the lineup. But just one game into the season, he was injured and forced to sit out for yet another season. Since then, Williams has returned to the Dolphins regular lineup and has helped to bring the team out of the basement of the league standings. Now a model player, he has slowly won back the love of the fans. But they know that with Ricky Williams, you can never be sure what will happen next.

Orange Bowl Antics

For Better and Worse

The Orange Bowl was the scene of mixed blessings for quarterbacks Joe Namath and Earl Morrall. Both men played in major championship games on the storied field in Miami and experienced crushing defeats that left a bitter aftertaste. But both men returned to achieve personal redemption.

An injured Namath led the undefeated Alabama Crimson Tide into the Orange Bowl against the Texas

Longhorns on New Year's Day 1965. This was the Alabama of Bear Bryant, with a record of 40–3 and two national championships in their last four seasons, going up against Darrell Royal's team, which won the national championship in 1963. The Longhorns didn't lack confidence, either; they entered the showdown with a 39–3–1 record in their previous four seasons.

Alabama fell behind as Texas took a 14–0 lead before Namath entered the game. The quarterback had injured his knee in practice in the days leading up to the game. He drove Alabama to its first touchdown, but the Crimson Tide trailed 21–7 at halftime. Alabama scored 10 unanswered points in the second half and drove to the Texas six-yard line with seven minutes left in the game. Three running plays advanced the ball to the one. On fourth down, Namath tried a quarterback sneak, and the pile moved forward. Namath claimed one official signaled touchdown, but the referee, who makes the final determination, said that Texas had stopped the Alabama quarterback just inches shy of the end zone.

Broadway Joe Returns to the Orange Bowl

Four seasons later, Namath led the AFL New York Jets into Miami to take on the NFL champion Baltimore Colts in Super Bowl III on January 12, 1969. Namath relished playing under the spotlight in the Big Apple. He took advantage of the Manhattan nightlife Monday through Saturday, and he led the Jets' powerful offense on Sundays. "Broadway Joe," as he was now called, guaranteed that the Jets, a prohibitive underdog in the game, would beat the champions of the senior league.

His counterpart that day was Earl Morrall, a 13-year veteran who had stepped in for an injured Johnny Unitas and guided the Colts to a 13–1 season. Baltimore moved the ball on offense throughout the first half, but with four drives deep into Jets territory, they had failed to generate either a touchdown or a field goal.

Morrall, who had his best season as a pro in 1968, had one of his worst days against the Jets. He was 6-of-17 passing for just 71 yards with three interceptions before being yanked by coach Don Shula late in the third quarter with the Colts trailing 13–0.

Meanwhile, Namath caught the NFL's best defense off guard by supplementing his passing attack with the running of Matt Snell on time-consuming drives that staked New York to a 16–0 lead that became a 16–7 win.

A Second and Third Act for Morrall

The pride and image of both leagues was on the line in Super Bowl III, and Morrall's poor play made him the goat of the football world.

In 1970, the merger of the two leagues was complete. The Colts advanced to Super Bowl V, again in Miami, as the new AFC champions to face the Dallas Cowboys. Morrall had resumed his status as the backup to Unitas. But Johnny U. was knocked from the game with a rib cage injury late in the first half with Baltimore trailing 13–6.

On the final possession of the half, Morrall completed passes of 26 and 21 yards on a drive to the Dallas two-yard line. But as they had done against the Jets on the same field two years earlier, Baltimore, with Morrall at the helm, failed to score on four tries.

With the monkey still on his back, a third-quarter drive also ended in disaster. A drive to the Dallas 15 ended when Morrall was intercepted in the end zone. Finally, Morrall engineered another drive, courtesy of a Dallas turnover, that tied the score at 13 with 7:35 left to play. Luckily for Morrall, Dallas quarterback Craig Morton was having a career-worst day of his own. On the Cowboys' final possession, Morton threw his third interception of the day, which gave Baltimore the ball deep in Dallas territory with less than a minute left in the game. A few plays later, Morrall held the ball for kicker Jim O'Brien, who split the uprights from 32 yards out to give the Colts—and Earl Morrall—a world championship.

Super Bowl V was not to be Morrall's last positive experience at the Orange Bowl. He was signed by the Dolphins in 1972 and stepped in for an injured Bob Griese. He won all nine of his starts, plus another in the playoffs, in Miami's "Perfect Season."

Morrall stayed with the Dolphins through 1976 and was a member of their 1973 championship team as well. He later served as a mentor and quarterback coach when Howard Schnellenberger took over the University of Miami program in 1979.

Outmanned But Not Outplayed

The national championship was not on the line when number-six Kansas played undefeated Penn State in the Orange Bowl on New Year's Day 1969. The Nittnay Lions, led by third-year coach Joe Paterno, were ranked third. It was a relatively well-played game between two evenly matched teams. Kansas scored first, but Penn State answered as the teams went into halftime tied at seven.

The Jayhawks went ahead in the fourth quarter when Don Shaklin's 47-yard punt return set up a one-yard touchdown by John Riggins. The extra point gave Kansas a 14–7 lead.

Late in the fourth quarter, Penn State blocked a punt and took over at midfield with a little over a minute remaining. On their team's first play, Penn State quarterback Chuck Burkhart hit halfback Bob Campbell, who was tackled at the three. As the teams headed downfield, Kansas sent substitutions for its final goal-line stand of the game. Nobody, including the officials, seemed to notice that the Jayhawks had 12 defenders.

The extra man helped as Penn State was stopped for no gain on two running plays. Still no flag. On third down, Burkhart ran a naked bootleg and scored the first touchdown of his career to cut the deficit to 14–13 with nine seconds left. Paterno told his troops that if they faced such a situation, they'd go for the two-point conversion and the win. But Burkhart's pass to Campbell was deflected by a Kansas defender, and it seemed that Kansas had won.

Finally, after four plays with an extra defender, the officials took notice of the extra Jayhawks player and called the penalty. Now, with the ball moved up to the one-yard line, Campbell scored on a sweep to give Penn State a 15–14 win.

When he was interviewed after the game, the official who called the penalty said he had noticed the extra man before the ball was snapped because his responsibility on the five-man crew was to count the players on every play—well, *almost* every play.

Tampa Bay Buccaneers
The Buccaneers' First Remains Their Best

Some people never get over their first love. In Tampa Bay's case, they have never had a player as good as their first-ever selection in the college draft. The team struck gold with its first draft pick, Lee Roy Selmon. Selected first overall in 1976, Selmon played at a Hall of Fame level from his first snap until injuries forced a premature end to his career in 1984 at age 30. In between, the consensus All-American from Oklahoma, who also won the Outland and Lombardi trophies his senior year, was selected to six Pro Bowls, named first-team All-Pro three times and voted the NFL Defensive Player of the Year in 1979.

Football was in Selmon's genes. In 1973, he started on the same line alongside his older brothers, Lucious and Dewey, both of whom also earned All-American honors. Dewey was chosen by the Bucs in the second round of the 1976 draft and started for several seasons at linebacker. Lee Roy captained a unit that for several seasons during his career was ranked at or near the top of the league's defenses. His best season occurred in 1979, when the Bucs allowed the fewest points in the NFL.

Selmon was active in local charities during his playing days and remained involved in community affairs after he retired. He joined the athletic staff at the University of South Florida and eventually became the school's athletic director. He owns several steakhouses that bear his name, as does a local road, the Lee Roy Selmon Crosstown Expressway. The Bucs retired Selmon's number 63 shortly after he retired, and in 1995, he was elected to the Pro Football Hall of Fame. Selmon stands alongside Don Shula and Bobby Bowden as one of the Sunshine State's most distinguished and beloved sports heroes.

Three That Got Away

The Bucs invested three high draft picks on quarterbacks Doug Williams (round one, 1977), Steve Young (round one, 1984 USFL supplemental) and Trent Dilfer (round one, 1994) with the hope that these strong-armed college signal callers could lead the franchise to its first Super Bowl. All three justified that faith by leading their teams to Super Bowl wins, with Williams and Young walking off the field with MVP honors.

The only problem was that none of those three winning teams were the Bucs. Williams left Tampa in 1983 after five roller-coaster seasons to join the Oklahoma Outlaws of the new United States Football League.

The league folded after three seasons, and Williams returned to the NFL in 1986 as a backup to Jay Schroeder with the Washington Redskins.

It appeared that Williams' career as a starter was over, but he had impressed head coach Joe Gibbs in several relief appearances in place of the sporadic Schroeder during the 1987 regular season and was tabbed as the Redskins starter for the playoffs. He responded by throwing for a Super Bowl record 340 yards and four touchdowns in a 35–10 win over the Denver Broncos in Super Bowl XXII.

After two grueling years in Tampa, Young was dealt to the San Francisco 49ers, where he apprenticed under the legendary Joe Montana for a few seasons. When Young stepped in for an injured Montana in 1991, he was so impressive that San Francisco decided to trade Montana, and Young was the starter until he retired nine years later. But in 1994, the former BYU star led San Francisco to the best record in pro football and capped off the season by throwing for a record six touchdowns in a 49–26 win over San Diego in Super Bowl XXIX.

It was particularly galling for Bucs fans when Dilfer, who they were all to happy to see leave after he was granted free agent status following the 1999 season, returned to Tampa as the starter for the Baltimore Ravens in Super Bowl XXXV against the Giants. There was no comparison between the Washington and San Francisco offensive talent that Williams and Young enjoyed compared to the "tools" that Dilfer had to work with.

At one point in the 2000 regular season, Baltimore went five consecutive games without scoring a touchdown. Dilfer replaced an ineffective Tony Banks midway through the season and led the Ravens to a 7–1 record and then four more victories in the playoffs, including a 34–7 rout over New York at Raymond James Stadium.

McKay Tries to Do the Impossible

A good lawyer doesn't put a witness on the stand unless he knows what is going to be said. In the world of sports, an owner doesn't hire a coach unless he knows what he is getting. In selecting John McKay as his first coach in 1976, owner Hugh Culverhouse knew he was getting the finest college coach in the nation. In the previous decade, McKay had built the University of Southern California program into the preeminent Division I program in college football. His Trojan teams won four national championships and had a record of 127–40–8.

The West Virginia native and graduate of the University of Oregon looked forward to the challenge of building the expansion Buccaneers into one of the NFL's elite teams. It proved a daunting task—the team lost its first 26 games, a league record that still stands. McKay was as demanding as any coach, but he also had a biting sense of humor. At one point during the "record-setting" losing streak, he was asked by a reporter about the offense's execution. McKay responded, "I'm for it."

While McKay was building the Bucs into a solid team defensively, what little punch they had on offense was supplied by the their second and third first-round picks. Tailback Ricky Bell, who McKay had coached at USC, was selected in 1977, and a year later, Doug Williams, a standout at Grambling, was tabbed to be the Bucs' quarterback of the future.

From Chumps to Division Champs

Just two years after their losing streak ended, the Bucs shocked the sports world by winning their first five games of the 1979 season—and they were 7–2 by November. But the offense went flat, and not even the NFL's best defense could prevent a second-half slide that had the Bucs facing a must-win situation in week 16 against Kansas City. Playing before a sparse crowd at Tampa Stadium in a heavy rain, Ricky Bell ran for 138 yards on 39 carries, and the Bucs closed the season as NFC Central Division champions with a 3–0 win over the Chiefs.

The Bucs Ring Their Bell

A week later, in their first-ever playoff game, the Bucs again relied on the running of Bell to get them past Philadelphia, winning with a score of 24–17. Bell ran for 142 yards on 38 carries and reached the end zone twice in the first half, which was one more touchdown than Tampa Bay had scored in their last three regular season games.

The Dream Season Ends

Another driving rainstorm, along with the Los Angeles Rams defense, doused the Bucs' dreams of meeting Pittsburgh in Super Bowl XIV. In one of the all-time defensive struggles in history, neither team scored a touchdown, but the Rams offense outgained the Bucs 369 yards to 177. The Bucs were eliminated 9–0, courtesy of three Frank Corral field goals.

Culverhouse Opens His Wallet

Some fans and media expressed the opinion that Bucs owner Hugh Culverhouse was a cheapskate, but his defenders claimed that he would do whatever he could to win. Did he not make head coach John McKay a substantial offer when he lured the college legend away from USC? In 1991, he also pursued Bill Walsh, the former head coach and architect of San Francisco's dynasty of the 1980s and '90s, but he was unable to entice the three-time Super Bowl champion.

And, in the fall and winter of 1991–92, he courted Bill Parcells, who at the time was one year removed from his second Super Bowl championship with the Giants. Parcells left the Giants, citing health concerns after New York won its second championship in five years. Culverhouse believed that he had made Parcells an offer—a five-year, $6.5 million deal—and that Parcells had accepted it, which would have made the coach the highest paid in the league, only to have Parcells change his mind. Parcells said he had weighed the offer but never accepted it.

Making a Big Splash

After a great career with the Florida Gators, wide receiver Jacquez Green was drafted by the Bucs in the second round of the 1998 NFL draft. He became a starter and made more than 50 receptions in two of his four seasons before leaving via free agency.

Green's first game was one he'd never forget. He caught two passes from quarterback Trent Dilfer and returned four kickoffs and two punts in a 23–15 loss to the Packers at Lambeau Field.

The play that made the day special came in the fourth quarter. With his team trailing Green Bay 23–0, Green took a Sean Landeta punt on the Bucs five-yard line and returned it 95 yards for a touchdown. It was only the fourth punt return for a touchdown in team history.

Where's Pat Sajak When You Need Him?

No one knows if former Buccaneer fullback Mike Alstott was a fan of the television game show *Wheel of Fortune,* but there was a time during his rookie season when he would have gladly asked Pat Sajak and Vanna White for another "T."

There are dozens of players in NFL history who rose from obscurity to greatness. Through hard work and spectacular play, they forced the coaches and their fellow players to take notice. It's not uncommon for the entire staff to take them for granted initially; most rookies who report to training camp get cut.

Seldom, however, would a second-round pick fall into that category. Yet, when Alstott joined the team after a stellar career at Purdue, the equipment staff actually had his named spelled wrong—Alsott—on the back of his jersey for the first two games of his rookie season. Alstott made sure that anyone who saw him play, or played against him, would easily remember his rather unchallenging two-syllable name. With six trips to the Pro Bowl, six playoff seasons and a Super Bowl championship, he no longer required the services of Pat and Vanna.

Dungy's D Nearly Stops the Greatest Show on Turf

Tampa Bay Buccaneers coach Tony Dungy made his reputation as a defensive guru. His genius was never more apparent than in the 1999 NFC championship game against the St. Louis Rams.

The Rams had one of the greatest offensive teams in NFL history, and the unit was given the moniker "the Greatest Show on Turf." Led by quarterback Kurt Warner, the Rams averaged 33 points per game in the regular season and had scored at least 30 points in seven consecutive games entering the playoff showdown against the Bucs. The winner would meet the Tennessee Titans in Super Bowl XXXIV in Atlanta.

Entering the game, Tampa had held 11 of its last 12 opponents to 20 points or less. Four Bucs defenders made the Pro Bowl as part of the NFL's third-best defense. Defensive tackle Warren Sapp, linebackers Hardy Nickerson and Derrick Brooks, safety John Lynch and their teammates stepped up their game.

All-purpose and All-Pro running back Marshall Faulk, who had gained more than 1000 yards both running and pass receiving that year, was held to

44 yards rushing on 17 carries, and he gained only five more yards on three receptions. Warner, the league's MVP that year, threw three interceptions and just one touchdown pass. Unfortunately, it was the game-winning score. With the Bucs clinging to a 6–5 lead, Warner hit Rickey Proehl with 4:44 remaining for the 11–6 win.

Even in defeat, the defense had a lot to be proud of. From 1999 through 2001, the Rams scored more than 500 points in an unprecedented three consecutive seasons. To appreciate what the Tampa Bay unit did in that NFC title game, consider that only five times during that 55-game span, including the playoffs, were the Rams held to fewer than 20 points. Dungy's defense was responsible for two of those efforts.

Gruden Gets Caught in the Perfect Storm

When Jon Gruden accepted the head coaching job with the Buccaneers in 2002, he knew that he was taking over a talented team that had become consistent winners, but it was also a team that many football fans, the media and the rest of the NFL believed had not reached its full potential under coach Tony Dungy. The low-key Dungy, of whom it was said, "He's too nice," was fired following the 2001 season.

Gruden, who had fielded playoff teams in his last two seasons in Oakland, was considered an offensive genius, but he wanted out from under the oppressive thumb of Raiders owner Al Davis. Thanks to Davis, both the Bucs and Gruden got their wish—but it would cost them down the line. In exchange for releasing

Gruden from his contract, Tampa Bay agreed to give Oakland two number-one and two number-two draft picks, plus a reported $8 million.

Gruden set a different tone than Dungy had, and the Bucs responded with a franchise best 12–4 record as well as a 48–21 victory over the Raiders in Super Bowl XXXVII. But the euphoria didn't last long. The Bucs had a team of talented veterans, but the constraints of the salary cap made it impossible to keep some of the players who had played a key role in their Super Bowl run. And, because of the draft picks they had given to Oakland to get Gruden, they had a much tougher task adding young talent.

Tampa Bay had back-to-back losing seasons in 2003 and 2004, failing to make the playoffs both times. Gruden fielded three winners from 2005 to 2008, but those teams were never considered Super Bowl contenders, and he was fired following the 2008 campaign.

Incidentally, the NFL no longer allows the trading of players or draft picks for non-players.

The Historic Drought Ends

Returning a kickoff for a touchdown is uncommon. Teams consider themselves fortunate if a return specialist can score at least one touchdown in a season, but rarely does a team go more than two seasons without accomplishing the feat. So as the years progressed, NFL observers thought it was odd that no Buccaneers kick returner had ever reached the end zone.

This is all the more remarkable when you consider that the team has had eight head coaches who took 10 teams to the playoffs, including one Super Bowl. The Buccaneers had scored 8455 points by every conceivable method except kickoff return and the dropkick.

The drought actually lasted three games shy of 32 full seasons. In a December 16, 2007, game against the Atlanta Falcons at Raymond James Stadium, Michael Spurlock made Buccaneers history when he returned kicker Morten Andersen's kickoff 90 yards for a touchdown.

What took 497 regular games plus 14 playoff games to happen once is now an annual occurrence. Since Spurlock broke the ice, two other Buccaneers returners have gone "coast to coast." Clifton Smith (2008) and Sammie Stroughter (2009) both returned kicks 97 yards for scores to join Spurlock in a very exclusive club. With his place in the team record book becoming cramped, Spurlock returned a kick 89 yards for a score in 2010 against Atlanta. He is now the only Buc to have returned two kickoffs for a touchdown.

Lynch Is Already in the Hall, Sort Of

Former Buccaneers defensive back John Lynch went to five Pro Bowls during his 11 years in Tampa and closed his career with four consecutive Pro Bowl appearances with the Denver Broncos. Given his stellar play for two teams, including a Super Bowl championship with the Bucs, induction into the Pro Football Hall of Fame should be a mere formality.

But few people know that Lynch is already in another professional sports Hall of Fame—though not as an inductee. The Bucs' 1993 third-round pick out of Stanford was also an excellent baseball player in high school and college. NFL fans know that Lynch was quite a hitter, but he made his mark in baseball as a pitcher. Lynch holds the distinction of throwing the first pitch in the history of the Florida Marlins baseball organization.

The pitching prospect was selected by the Marlins in the second round of the 1992 amateur draft and took the mound later that year to pitch the first game for the Marlins' Class A team, the Erie Sailors. Because of this, his jersey is in the Baseball Hall of Fame in Cooperstown.

Leading with Brains and Brawn

From his linebacker position, Derrick Brooks spent 14 years with the Buccaneers, blocking the pathway to the end zone from opposing players with as much skill as any defender in NFL history. He was an 11-time Pro Bowler and was the NFL's Defensive Player of the Year during the Bucs' Super Bowl championship season of 2002. The future Pro Football Hall of Famer (he'll be eligible for the first time in 2014) was a model of consistency on the field and a role model off it. Brooks first gained national attention in 1990 when *USA Today* named him the National Defensive Player of the Year following his senior season at Washington High School in Pensacola.

Brooks earned a bachelor's degree and a master's degree from Florida State, where he was a two-time All-American linebacker and a member of the school's 1993 national championship team. Since before his retirement, Brooks has been involved in improving education at both the scholastic and the college level. He was appointed to the Board of Trustees at Florida State in 2003 by then-governor Jeb Bush, and in 2007, he cofounded the Brooks-DeBartolo Collegiate High School in Tampa. Brooks-DeBartolo is a charter school with a mission to prepare students for college by challenging them with a rigorous curriculum consisting of dual-enrollment and advanced-placement courses. Since the school opened, it has boasted a graduation rate of 100 percent and has had graduates accepted to such prestigious universities as Harvard and MIT.

Jacksonville Jaguars

Hungry for Pro Football

Pro football was a long time coming to Jacksonville. The city "Where Florida Begins" had been home to the Sharks of the WFL in the mid-1970s, and the Bulls, who played for the final two years of the USFL in the early 1980s. At various times, other franchises such as the Baltimore Colts and Houston Oilers flirted with the idea of relocating to Jacksonville.

The city had also proved its bona fides at the college level. It hosted the postseason college bowl game, the Gator Bowl. Jacksonville also played host to the "World's

Largest Cocktail Party"—the annual game between the universities of Florida and Georgia.

In 1989, a group of local business leaders formed a group called Touchdown Jacksonville with the intention of recruiting enough local support to approach the NFL about granting them an expansion franchise. Finally, after years of negotiating, which included more than $100 million in promised renovations to the Gator Bowl, and keeping the local population enthused, the group, now headed by J. Wayne Weaver, accomplished its goal. On November 20, 1993, the NFL announced that Jacksonville would be home to the league's 30th and newest team. The Jags would be making their debut in 1995, along with the Carolina Panthers, who had become the NFL's 29th team a month earlier.

Coughlin Brings a Winning Tradition

Boston College coach Tom Coughlin was a solid choice to be the team's first head coach and general manager. Coughlin had apprenticed under Bill Parcells in New York and saw how Parcells and GM George Young constructed two Super Bowl–championship teams.

Prior to Coughlin's arrival in Boston, BC had four consecutive losing seasons. Coughlin turned the program around, including a big win over then–number one rated Notre Dame in 1993. The Eagles handed the Fighting Irish their only loss for the season, which ultimately cost Lou Holtz's squad the national championship.

In Jacksonville, Coughlin's first personnel moves proved to be shrewd. He traded for Green Bay backup quarterback Mark Brunell, drafted offensive tackle Tony Boselli and signed free agent wide receiver Jimmy Smith. All three players appeared in several Pro Bowls and were mainstays of Jacksonville's early playoff teams.

What Sophomore Jinx?

Having learned from the Tampa franchise's embarrassing start two decades earlier, the NFL granted Jacksonville and Carolina additional premium draft picks in the annual selection of college talent in the hope of jumpstarting their paths to respectability. Still, nobody expected both teams to have winning records, let alone make it to the playoffs in their second seasons. But they did.

The Jaguars' 1996 season started on a high note when they beat the defending AFC champion Pittsburgh Steelers at home, 24–7. But the rest of September and October featured just two more wins, and the Jags stood 3–6.

Luck finally started to work in the Jags' favor as Jacksonville won six of its last seven games, none by more than a touchdown. But a happy ending to their Cinderella season wasn't assured until the dying moments of the last game of the regular season at home against Atlanta. After the Falcons had closed to within 17–19 earlier in the fourth quarter, the usually sure-footed kicker, Morten Andersen, missed a 30-yard field goal attempt with four seconds remaining to send the sold-out crowd into a frenzy and their team into the playoffs with a 9–7 record.

Buffaloing the Bills

Nothing was going to come easy for the upstarts from North Florida, especially against the veteran Buffalo Bills, who had never lost a playoff game at home. Playing a team that still had many of its veterans left from their four Super Bowl runs, the Jags waged a furious contest against the Bills that saw the lead change hands or the score tied seven times.

Up until the Buffalo game, veteran running back Natron Means was having an unspectacular season. He ran for just 507 yards for a paltry 3.3 average.

But Means rose to the occasions, rumbling for 175 yards on 31 carries that included a 62-yard burst and a scoring run of 30 yards. Mark Brunell added 239 yards in the air and kicker Mike Hollis added the last of his three field goals with three minutes left to secure the final margin of victory, 30–27. Next stop, Denver.

A Mile-High Mugging

In John Elway, Denver had one of the all-time great quarterbacks. With the exception of San Francisco's Joe Montana, no signal caller provided as many late-game theatrics as the 14-year veteran out of Stanford. But few people outside Jacksonville expected the 1996 Broncos, with an AFC best 13–3 record, to need Elway's special talent on this day—especially in the friendly confines of Mile High Stadium.

Two first-quarter touchdowns gave the Broncos a 12–0 lead. But then the Jags, again behind the running of Means and the ball-control passing of Brunell, took control. By the fourth quarter, three Mike Hollis field goals and touchdowns by Means and receiver Keenan McCardell gave the Jags a 23–12 lead. The Broncos were shocked, as were their 80,000 faithful, who had not seen their team lose at home that season.

The Denver offense regained its footing in the fourth quarter as running back Terrell Davis capped a drive with a two-yard scoring run, and then ran for the two-point conversion that pulled the Broncos to within 23–20.

In what was arguably their finest hour, Brunell and the offense answered the Broncos with a touchdown drive of their own. Jimmy Smith hauled in a 16-yard pass from Brunell, and Hollis added the extra point for a 30–20 lead. The Broncos scored again, but the Jags hung on for a 30–27 win. They were just one game away from the Super Bowl.

From Mile High to Earthbound

When the 1996 season started, none of Florida's three NFL teams were picked to make the Super Bowl. Even so, if a miracle were to occur, most experts said it would come from farther south, from two-time Super Bowl champion coach Jimmy Johnson and his future Hall of Fame quarterback, Dan Marino.

With two hair-raising playoff road victories against more experienced, veteran teams under their belt, the

Big Cats were starting to believe they had what it took to meet the Packers in Super Bowl XXXI. Jacksonville fans were getting primed for an eight-hour road trip across the Panhandle on Interstate 10 to the Superdome in New Orleans. But first they'd need another road victory, this time against the Patriots in Foxboro, Massachusetts. On a bitterly cold day, the Jags couldn't get anything going on offense. While the defense held the Patriots to just 13 first downs, they couldn't overcome four offensive turnovers, the last of which, a fumble, was returned for a touchdown. An otherwise great season ended on a bitter and frustrating note with a final score of 20–6.

The Titans Ruin the Best Season

With John Elway retired from Denver, the maturing, now seasoned playoff Jaguars believed the Super Bowl was a realistic expectation for the 1999 season. The roster featured seven players who were voted to the Pro Bowl. Mark Brunell guided a balanced attack, throwing to Jimmy Smith and Keenan McCardell, who were as good as any receiving tandem in the league. On the ground, Jacksonville's one-two punch of James Stewart and rookie first-round pick Fred Taylor added balance. On the other side of the ball, defensive end Tony Brackens, linebacker Kevin Hardy and safety Carnell Lake had Pro Bowl seasons and led a unit that proved to be the toughest to score on in the NFL, allowing just 217 points.

The only blemishes en route to a league, and franchise, best 14–2 record were two losses to the Tennessee Titans. In a week three game at home, the Jags blew a 17–7 fourth-quarter lead and lost 20–19. Eleven consecutive wins later, Coughlin led the team into Nashville looking for revenge against their intra-division rival, which was also playoff bound at 11–3. Tennessee dominated from the outset. Steve McNair threw for 291 yards, and Eddie George ran for 102 more as the Titans gained 476 total yards for a 41–14 win.

The Jags returned home and closed out the season with a solid 24–7 win over Cincinnati, edging out the Titans for the AFC South division title. Two weeks later, they hosted Miami in the divisional round of the playoffs. The Jags were unstoppable both on the ground and in the air as they gained 520 yards and sent coach Jimmy Johnson and quarterback Dan Marino into retirement with a 62–7 win.

All that stood between Jacksonville and a Super Bowl showdown with the St. Louis Rams were the Titans, who not only swept the regular season series but had held the Jags to fewer than 20 points in their last three meetings.

That looked like it was going to change as Brunell connected with tight end Kyle Brady for a seven-yard touchdown pass in the first quarter to take the lead 7–0. After Tennessee tied the score, Stewart's 33-yard scoring run sent the Jags into halftime with a 14–10 advantage.

Once again, Tennessee controlled the second half and beat the Jags for a third time with a score of 33–14. It was a disappointing end to an otherwise great season.

Chapter Three

The Great American Race

The First Organized Stock Car Race

Travel five miles north of the famous Daytona International Speedway and you will come to the place where organized stock car racing began. Ormond Beach offered the perfect conditions for car racing—the beach had a natural incline that made it easy for drivers to handle the cars in turns, it was wide enough to allow more than 10 cars to race at one time and, most importantly, the quartz in the sand made it pack down hard enough for the tires to grip. The beach quickly became known as a place to attempt speed records.

Seizing upon the potential of the terrain, several teams gathered on the shores of Ormond Beach in 1903 and attempted to set a new land speed record, but only two of the vehicles were considered race cars, one nicknamed "Bullet" and the other "Pirate."

The event, held from March 26 to 28, was organized by William J. Morgan and was only supposed to be an attempt at a land speed record, but Morgan saw an opportunity to bring in more spectators by having the two cars race each other out on the beach. The two vehicles belted down the sand, and the first-ever stock car race was born. After that event, Ormond Beach became *the* place for stock car aficionados to test their cars against the region's best, and it wasn't until the the raceway at Daytona Beach opened in 1959 that Ormond Beach fell out of favor. But it was there along the coast of Florida that all the early heroes of the sport got their start.

The Birth of NASCAR

In December 1948, Bill France founded the National Association for Stock Car Auto Racing (NASCAR) in Daytona Beach, unifying a small group of sanctioning bodies that had sprouted up when Detroit began building newer, faster cars after World War II.

France, who was born and raised in Washington, DC, was a car enthusiast his entire life. As a teenager, he raced the family Model T and eventually opened his own service station. In the 1930s, he moved to Florida with his wife and young son. He became a part of the racing scene in Daytona Beach as both a driver and race promoter. Over the next decade, France's stature and influence grew. He was determined to bring uniformity in race procedure and technical rules to the sport on a national scale.

While other racing associations focused on building cars for maximum speed, France realized that this would only attract a limited number of spectators who had a genuine interest in cars. For his new association, France wanted to appeal to the average

American family—people who would relate more to street-legal, family-style sedans than the super cars of Formula 1. From NASCAR's humble beginnings through its evolution into a successful multibillion-dollar business, France had the right idea in targeting the general public.

The First Daytona 500

From 1948 until 1959, stock car racing in Florida really did not have a home of its own. Bill France had been operating his races on the beach in Daytona, but as the sport grew in popularity, he knew he would need a new home in order to showcase his events. He risked everything and decided to build a new track in the middle of Florida's swampland, some four miles from the beach where he had first organized races. Critics said it would never work and that no one would travel to a swamp to watch stock cars race, but France did not listen.

When the Daytona raceway was completed, France had built a 2.5-mile track the like of which the United States had never seen. It would allow car manufacturers and racing teams to push the limits of construction and speed in order to get the most out of their cars. By January 1959, the Daytona Motor Speedway was complete and ready for its first event.

That year, all the major American automobile companies released their newest and most powerful cars to date. Ford introduced a new version of the Thunderbird, GM/Pontiac introduced the new Catalina, and Chevrolet brought in their new Impala. The manufacturers flocked to Daytona to show off their latest cars, and a week before the race was even set to start, all of downtown Daytona was draped with automobile company logo banners and signs announcing to the world that stock car racing had arrived on the scene. France had been able to wrestle some money out of the car companies and put it toward the prize money for the winning team.

France had built the speedway not only with seats surrounding the track from the outside, but he had also created a vast infield where drivers and fans could mingle together freely before the race. Small portable villages full of race fans sprang up before each race, with people bringing their vans and RVs and setting up barbecues. Fans even went so far as to place their lawn chairs on the trucks and camper roofs in order to get a better view of the action on the track.

The first Daytona 500 (200 laps on the 2.5-mile oval track), which took place on February 22, 1959, received so much pre-race hype that even legendary CBS news commentator Walter Cronkite reported from the venue on the new craze sweeping across the United States. When the cars got the green flag, the crowds marveled at the speeds the drivers reached as they hit the steep embankments going over 120 miles per hour. The first heat was a tight race that came down to a photo finish, but race officials could not announce a winner because it was so close. It took over 60 hours to analyze the film and come up with the decision that Lee Petty's number 42 Oldsmobile had barely edged Johnny Beauchamp's Ford as the checkered flag came down. That finish-line photo from the initial "Great American Race" is one of the most famous in stock car history.

Lee Petty's winnings amounted to $19,500, not much in comparison to the $1.5 million that today's Daytona 500 winners take home, but an excellent payday for a sport just making its way into the mainstream. Within a month or two of the first Daytona 500, construction plans for new raceways began springing up across the southern states in places like Atlanta and Charlotte, and even out west in California.

It was fitting that Lee Petty won the inaugural Daytona 500. He was one of the sport's pioneers, and he was also the patriarch of one of the most famous racing dynasties. His son, Richard, would go on to win the Daytona 500 a record seven times and become the most successful driver in stock car history.

Daytona Tragedy

On February 18, 2001, when the green flag dropped for the start of the Daytona 500, fans were to witness some of the most intense hours of side-by-side racing ever seen on the speedway. From the moment the cars pulled off their lines, they stayed in a tight pack, creating an exciting race for fans and a nervous one for the teams in the pits. Those tight conditions eventually resulted in a spectacular crash that took out a total of 19 cars, highlighted by Tony Stewart's car careening skyward with the engine on fire.

"There was no getting through it. It was like a wall of cars," said driver Jeff Gordon.

After the mess of cars and debris had been cleared off the track, just a few drivers were left to finish the remaining laps. Coming into the last five laps, the entire race boiled down to two cars, those of Michael Waltrip and Dale Earnhardt Jr. They had just pulled away from a group of cars that included Dale Earnhardt Sr., Kenny Schrader, Sterling Marlin and Rusty Wallace. Many in the stands watched and hoped that Dale Sr. would make one of his patented moves to slingshot past the two leaders and bring home his third career Daytona 500 win.

His son, Dale Jr., and Waltrip were still far out in front, and fans were becoming impatient for the old veteran to make his move, but Dale Sr. continued to block the other cars in the pack from getting ahead. He began drifting a little toward the bottom of the track, where Sterling Marlin was holding his line going into Turn 3. Then Dale Sr.'s Chevy suddenly skidded down onto the apron of the track, fishtailing as it went. Rounding the corner out of control, the car's nose tilted toward the outside wall, and Ken Schrader came crashing into Dale Sr.'s passenger-side door. Traveling at a speed of around 180 miles per hour, Dale Sr.'s car slammed headfirst into the wall at Turn 4. The crash looked innocent enough when compared to the fiery spectacle earlier in the race, but when the vehicle finally came to a rest after sliding down into the infield, there was no movement inside the car.

Television cameras continued to cover the race, and fans watched as Waltrip crossed the finish line for the victory. Waltrip went along through to the victory lane to celebrate, completely unaware that his friend was in trouble. As Waltrip took his victory lap, he had to pass the smoking wreckage of Earnhardt's car as emergency workers tried to free the veteran to save his life. But all the effort was for naught—Dale Sr. had died instantly upon impact with the wall. Waltrip, like most others on the track, had figured the crews were just having trouble getting the driver out of the car, so the celebrations continued. But when Waltrip sat down to give his press interview, he could tell something was wrong.

Dale Beaver, the trackside chaplain for the Winston Cup organization was hurried over to the infield emergency center. Beaver accompanied Dale Jr. and the rest of the family to the local hospital, where doctors delivered the horrible news that Dale Sr. was dead. Dr. Steve Bohannon, director of emergency medical services at Daytona Speedway, responded to the crash and confirmed that the driver had died instantly. He added that there were no visible signs of trauma on Dale Sr.'s face or body that would indicate how he died.

NASCAR president Mike Helton was given the task of relaying the news of Earnhardt's death to the public, saying, "Undoubtedly, this is one of the toughest announcements I've personally had to make. After the accident in Turn 4 at the end of the Daytona 500, we've lost Dale Earnhardt [Sr.]."

Bill France Jr., who succeeded his father as NASCAR president and served until 2000, added, "NASCAR has lost its greatest driver ever, and I personally have lost a great friend."

Since the opening of the Daytona speedway, there have been 26 deaths as a result of crashes. A few days after the crash, a report by Dr. Bohannon was released saying that Earnhardt's life might have been saved if he had been wearing a special head and neck brace called the HANS device. It was also later discovered that part of his seatbelt had broken, which may also have contributed to his death by allowing his body to move forward and his chin to hit the steering wheel, fracturing his spine at the base of his skull.

On February 21, 2001, Dale Earnhardt Sr. was laid to rest.

A Legend on Every Surface

Robert Glen "Junior" Johnson is a driving legend and one of those characters from a bygone era during the early days of stock car racing. Johnson was born in Wilkes County, North Carolina, in 1931. The superior driving skills he employed to win the Daytona 500 in 1960 were honed running moonshine on the back roads of the Tar Heel State, where he became a local legend by consistently outrunning and evaded law enforcement in hot, often high-speed pursuits.

"Moonshiners put more time, energy, thought and love into their cars than any racer ever will," Johnson said. "Lose on the track and you go home. Lose with a load of whiskey and you go to jail."

Johnson joined the stock car circuit in 1955 and was an immediate success. He won five races in his first year of racing and was a frequent visitor to the winner's circle through 1960. Hall of Fame driver Ned

Jarrett considered Johnson one of the greatest drivers on dirt.

But in 1956, this bootlegger's boy had his career interrupted when federal agents caught him working at his father's still. Johnson was convicted of moonshining and sent to federal prison, where he served 11 months of a two-year sentence. In 1986, he was granted a pardon from President Ronald Reagan for his federal moonshining conviction.

At Daytona in 1960, Johnson pioneered the tactic that he successfully used to win the 500 despite driving a car that was considerably slower than the fastest cars in the field that year. He had discovered during qualifying heats that if he pulled up close, to within a few inches directly behind the competition, he could keep pace with the bigger and faster vehicles. This was the beginning of the technique of drafting, which quickly became a necessity in every driver's repertoire.

Johnson retired in 1966 but stayed in racing and became one of the most successful team owners in history. From 1976 to 1985, Cale Yarborough (1976, 1977, 1978) and Darrell Waltrip (1981, 1982, 1985) both won three Winston Cup championships driving under the Johnson banner.

Fearless Fireball

Those who first learn about NASCAR pioneer Glenn "Fireball" Roberts are surprised to discover that he didn't acquire his nickname as a result of his fearless, crowd-pleasing style behind the steering wheel during races. A native of Tavares, Roberts began racing on the sands at Daytona in 1948 when he was just 17. His moniker, pronounced *Fah-bawl*, came as a result of his exploits as a pitcher on his American Legion baseball team.

Roberts attended the University of Florida in pursuit of a degree in mechanical engineering but dropped out to race cars on the oval on a full-time basis in 1950. He spent six years racing modified stock cars before joining the Grand National circuit in 1956. During that time, Fireball became a fan favorite, with a driving style that has been described as "win, wreck or blow." That daring reputation served Roberts well as he finished in the top five 45 percent of the time. The biggest of his 33 wins came at the 1962 Daytona 500.

Sadly, at the 1964 World 600 in Charlotte, North Carolina, Roberts crashed into a wall while trying to avoid a collision that involved other cars and died as a result of his injuries. He was just 35.

Bobby Allison: A Giant Among Racing's Giants

Miami native Bobby Allison was racing cars while he was still a teen growing up in South Florida during the 1950s. After graduating from high school in 1955, he became more serious about a career in stock car racing and eventually moved to Montgomery, Alabama, with his brother, Donnie, and a friend. They became known in stock car racing circles as the Alabama Gang.

The move to Montgomery launched one of the greatest careers in the history of competitive car racing.

Allison, who also worked as a mechanic and engine tester, accumulated 84 wins as a driver and ranks third on the all-time list of victories. He won the Daytona 500 in 1978, 1982 and 1988. For his 1978 win, Allison worked his way up from 33rd place to take the checkered flag and end a 67-race winless streak. His third win at Daytona was also noteworthy because the 50-year-old not only became the oldest driver to win the race, but the second-place finisher that day was his son, Davey. In 1992, the younger Allison eventually added his name to the list of winners of NASCAR's most prestigious event.

A few months after his final win at Daytona, Bobby Allison was involved in a career-ending accident at Pocono Raceway in Pennsylvania. In 2011, he was enshrined along with the second class of inductees in the new NASCAR Hall of Fame in Charlotte, North Carolina.

Chapter Four

Homegrown Highlights

Fans of Florida's Major League Baseball teams haven't had too much to cheer about. Both the Marlins and the Rays have enjoyed a degree of success, but they didn't become big league clubs until the 1990s. Up until that time, the only baseball highlights that took place were in the Grapefruit League during spring training. But with the recent success of the Rays, along with the Marlins' two World Series championship teams, Floridians can enjoy quality baseball when the rest of the teams head north in April.

The Marlins Go Fishin'

Florida Marlin baseball is kind of like fishing for that dream giant marlin out on the open waters surrounding our beautiful coastline. Let us compare the seasons of the Marlins to the trials and triumphs of a fisherman.

Starting in 1993, the Marlins baseball club tossed out their line in an effort to win the World Series, as is the goal of every team, but like many young clubs and first casts, you often don't get anything back. The

Marlins failed to make the playoffs, so they cast out their line again the next season and again failed to even get a nibble of the playoffs. The same outcome continued over the next few seasons until the Marlins finally got their first playoff bite in 1997. The team pulled back on their reserve strength and just managed to hook the playoffs by catching the wild card spot. The Marlins were tough, hanging onto the line against San Francisco in the Division Series, but they easily pulled through that first challenge, sweeping the Giants in three games.

The struggle for the National League championship was a tougher one because the playoff-seasoned Atlanta Braves stood in the way. But the Marlins dug deep and found the strength to get through that series 4–2 and reel the World Series trophy that much closer to home. The Marlins were now in the final stages of the battle, and their opponents would be the American League champions, the Cleveland Indians. The Indians battled hard and forced the Marlins to fight through seven games, but they just managed to reel the championship in when Craig Counsell scored on Edgar Rentería's single in the bottom of the 11th inning for a 3–2 win. The Marlins could now hang the picture of the team holding their hard-won trophy in their parlor.

After the 1997 season, a violent storm whipped up and knocked several key players off the boat, lost forever in the troubled waters of financial losses. The team that reported to spring training trying to land the big catch looked far different than the previous one had. Yet, they cast their line out once more, but it just wasn't the same without the championship players they'd lost, and the Marlins could not even get a nibble of the playoffs for five straight seasons.

But in 2003, with a mixture of young, talented pitchers like Dontrelle Willis and Josh Beckett, along with quality veterans Mike Lowell and Ivan Rodriguez, the Marlins threw out their line and finally got a bite, just enough to hook them into the playoffs with another wild card berth courtesy of a 91–71 record. They dispatched the Giants in four games (3–1), held on with some luck against the Cubs and beat the favored Yankees in the World Series 4–2 to reel in their second championship trophy.

Since then, the Marlins have expectantly cast their line into each season but have not managed to return to the playoffs again and only once finished as high as second in the National League East. So, truly, the Florida Marlins are out there every season casting their line of hope into the season and waiting for a bite to get them into the playoffs. But once they get the World Series on the line, history has shown that they'll reel in their prized catch every time. But like fishing for marlin, sometimes the big one still gets away.

God Bless Steve Bartman

In every great tragedy played out on the baseball field that gets entered into the history books—like the Red Sox loss of Babe Ruth or a blown call by an umpire during a World Series—the team on the receiving end of that disaster will also immortalize that moment in the legends of their franchise. The event will be written about and, sometimes, like Bill Buckner's miss of the ball in 1986 that cost the Red Sox the World Series, it will enter into popular culture through references in books, movies and music. While some weep at the moment when the ball trickled through Bill Buckner's legs, others see that play and fondly remember the time that Mookie Wilson's ground ball slipped by Buckner and allowed their team to score the game-winning run. That costly error by the Red Sox first baseman was a factor in pushing the Mets on to the World Series championship. The Florida Marlins themselves were the beneficiaries of another team's bad luck during the 2003 National League championship against the Chicago Cubs in what would go down as one of the most famous moments in the sport's recent history.

The Marlins and the Cubs were locked in battle for the right to move on to the World Series, but by the end of the fifth game of the series, the Cubs had taken a 3–2 stranglehold and needed just one more win to head to the championship. Cubs fans could sense that their years of bad luck and disappointment were about to end. Barring a complete disaster, the Cubs just might hold on and win the team's first title since 1908.

The Marlins were backed into a corner but were not about to give up. Going into a must-win game six, the Marlins sent Carl Pavano to the mound to hold off the Cubs batters, but by the seventh inning, Pavano, along with relief pitchers Dontrelle Willis and Chad Fox, had allowed the Chicago batters to score three runs. Only two more innings and the Cubs would be on their way to the World Series.

At the top of the eighth, the Marlins already had one out but had managed to put outfielder Juan Pierre on second base. The Cubs were five outs away from the World Series. The Marlins Luis Castillo came to bat and knocked the ball sky high toward the left field corner. The ball looked to be headed into the stands, but Cubs left fielder Moises Alou keenly tracked the ball, hoping to get the out. Then it happened. Just as the ball was coming down, Alou jumped up to make the catch, but so did a number of nearby fans hoping to snag a souvenir. The scene almost played out in slow motion, with Alou leaping into the air, and the ball coming down into the stands and deflecting off the outstretched arms of one Steve Bartman.

Alou screamed to the umpire that he had been interfered with, but the play was called a foul and Castillo was allowed to continue his at bat. Although several fans had tried to do the exact same thing as Bartman, he was the one singled out by the fans and immediately became the target of a chorus of boos and hot dog wrappers. Park security escorted Bartman out of the stadium for his own safety.

When the game got underway after the delay, Mark Prior, the Cubs starter, walked Castillo on a ball four wild pitch, sending Juan Pierre to third. Ivan Rodriguez then stepped up to the plate and singled, driving in the first run of the inning. The Cubs continued to unravel. Miguel Cabrera hit an easy grounder to Alex Gonzalez, who mishandled the ball, allowing Cabrera to reach first to load the bases. Derrek Lee was up next and drove in two runs with a double to tie the score 3-3. Prior was relieved of duty, but it did nothing to stem the bleeding of runs. A sacrifice fly then put the Marlins ahead 4-3, and after the bases were loaded again on an intentional walk, Mike Mordecai blasted a bases-clearing double that put the Marlins up 7-3. Juan Pierre made it back to the batters box that inning and drove in Mordecai with a single to make it 8-3. Finally, Castillo, the batter who started the whole controversy, popped out to end the inning. The Marlins won 8-3, sending the series to a deciding seventh game.

The Marlins incredible, fan-aided comeback wasn't the main story of game six. Every television news program in the Windy City led with the story of Steve Bartman's "interference." A few minutes after the game ended, irate Cubs fans posted Bartman's address all over the Internet. Hostility toward the poor man grew so bad that six police cars were sent to his house to protect him and his family. The beleaguered fan issued an apology, but it did nothing to stop the constant barrage of hate directed toward him. Illinois governor Rod Blagojevich made the situation worse when he suggested that Bartman enter the witness protection program, while Florida governor Jeb Bush jokingly offered Bartman asylum.

For game seven, the Cubs tried to put the incident out of their minds while the Marlins went into the game riding the emotions of their great comeback. The Cubs sent their ace Kerry Wood to the mound, and the strategy seemed to work as they pulled ahead 5–3, but the Marlins battled back to win 9–6 and advance to their second Fall Classic.

While Bartman was considered Public Enemy No. 1 by his fellow Cubs fans, Marlins supporters could not thank him enough. He was sent so many gifts that he had to publicly request that any further offerings be donated to the Juvenile Diabetes Research Foundation.

The Florida Flamingos?

When it was announced in June 1991 that the city of Miami would be granted a Major League Baseball franchise, the search for an appropriate name for the club began. The team's name had to reflect the state it was in and also the area around the city—something that spoke to the unique nature of Florida and the character of the new team.

Working closely with Major League Baseball's design director Anne Occi, Marlins owner Wayne Huizenga took his time considering what name would best represent the team and its hometown. South Florida already had the Miami Dolphins, the university team in Gainesville had taken the name Gators, and the same year that the eventual Marlins started in the league in 1993, Florida's NHL team had taken the name Panthers. Occi and Huizenga brainstormed ideas but could not come up with anything that sounded right. With all the cool animal names taken, those that were left were hardly compelling: the Florida Manatees, the Florida Water Snakes, the Florida Old Timers?

"We considered calling the team the Florida Flamingos," recalled Huizenga. But the thought of players wearing pink pinstripe uniforms did not sit well with the marketing department. So Anne Occi spent some time along the Florida coastline taking in the cool teal blue of the ocean, then she noticed the teal color of the bottom of the swimming pools, the teal fountains throughout Miami's streets...and it clicked in her mind. Occi and a few executives from MLB went down to the library (no Wikipedia back then) and checked out the color of the marlin. Bingo—teal. The tough fish found off Florida's coast would be the new image for Florida's baseball team.

It was a risk for the conservative culture of baseball, but nothing spoke to the region and the city as well as the color teal and the fighting spirit of the marlin. Just imagine if the name Flamingos had stuck! *Shiver.*

Mermaids and Manatees

Baseball culture is generally conservative and heavy on tradition. The upper management of Major League Baseball has tried very hard to keep America's national pastime the same as it was over 100 years ago, and since those days, there has been little variation in the product that fans see when they venture down to the ballpark.

But South Florida is not a traditional baseball market. In order to survive in Miami, a team needs to be fresh, innovative and sexy. Now, you might say there is nothing sexy about baseball, and you would be right. But the Miami Heat have managed to turn every basketball game into an event by adding lights, music and, most of all, cheerleaders. The Dolphins also sex up their image with a group of lovely young women in scanty outfits.

Even though the Florida Marlins won a World Series title in 1997, by the year 2000, they were having trouble filling seats. The average attendance in 2002 only reached about 10,000 per game, and on bad nights, you could hear fans coughing in the stands. The Marlins marketing department needed to do something drastic to get fans in seats, so they used a time-tested marketing device proven to get results—sex.

With the debut of the Marlins Mermaids in 2003, the baseball team became the first in major league history to have a dance/cheer team. The contingent of sexy female dancers would entertain the fans before the start of each game with a raucous routine and would appear throughout the game whenever there was a lull in play.

The ploy seemed to work. The Marlins per-game average attendance jumped from 10,000 in 2002 to over 16,000 in 2003. Although the Mermaids managed to bring a few more people into the stands, their effect was minimal. The place where their influence could be seen was on the field. Call it a coincidence or possibly motivation, but the Marlins turned things around in 2003, finishing second in their division and earning the team their second trip to the playoffs in their history. The young women continued to cheer throughout the postseason, and the team continued to win.

The Marlins made it past the San Francisco Giants, and the Mermaids cheered them on. They made it past the Chicago Cubs to take the National League championship, and the women kept dancing. The team made it past the New York Yankees and took home their second World Series title. Not a bad accomplishment for a team that hadn't even finished fourth the year before.

But just two seasons later, the Marlins looked nothing like the team that had won a World Series, and attendance once again began to plummet. In 2008, their marketing department, always looking for something to get fans into seats, came up with the idea of having an all-male dance squad. But unlike the lovely and athletic female dancers, these men would be of the plus-size variety and go by the apt moniker, the Marlin Manatees.

"They're another team we're creating for weekend games to give the crowd a charge," Marlins vice president of marketing Sean Flynn said. "We're looking for big guys."

And the ploy seemed to work. Even before the Manatees made their first appearance, they were mentioned in newspapers as far away as China and had several requests for interviews from radio stations in Germany! Appearing only on Saturdays and Sundays, the Manatees were an instant hit with the fans. To this day, the rotund men of the Manatees continue to shake their bellies in support of their hometown team, and as much as you might want to turn away at the sight of a group of 300-pound guys dancing, you just cannot help but be taken in by the group's enthusiasm for their team and their city. The Marlins now also have a troupe of teenage dancers called the Marlin Minnows.

Local Boy Caps Hall of Fame at Home

When legendary slugger Wade Boggs joined the Tampa Bay Rays, then called the Devil Rays, in 1998, he was in the twilight of a Hall of Fame–caliber career. Rays management knew that they were getting a player way past his prime, but Boggs, who graduated from Plant High School in Tampa, had added value as a veteran player who could help the young rookies cope with the pressures of the big league. Joining the Rays in their first year of operation, Boggs' name also served as a way of getting fans in seats to see the veteran play a season or two before retiring.

Although Boggs did not help the Rays win a World Series or even make the playoffs during the two years he played before his hometown fans, his marquee value brought a level of class and attention to the team. On the field, Boggs did what he was supposed to and carried his share of the workload during games. Nothing spectacular happened in his first season with the club, and he finished with a .280 batting average. It was in his second season that he made history.

At the start of the 1999 season, the five-time American League batting champion's career hits total crept ever closer to the magical 3000 mark. He chipped away as the season progressed, and on August 7, during a game at Tropicana Field against the Cleveland

Indians, Boggs stepped up to the plate with 2999 career hits already under his belt. Now, throughout his career, most of those hits had come from singles, but for his 3000th hit, Boggs belted a Chris Haney pitch deep over the right field fence for a home run. Even before the ball had cleared the playing field, Rays fans were on their feet, cheering for the veteran player as he started his trot around the bases. When he arrived at home plate, Boggs fell to his knees and kissed the plate in celebration.

When Boggs scored his 3000th career hit, he had 118 career home runs, 575 doubles, 66 triples and 2240 singles! The home run was the crowning achievement as well as the final highlight of his career. One month later, Boggs injured his knee and was forced to retire. He ended his career with 3010 career hits. The home run ball for hit 3000 was caught by a fan and returned to Boggs after the game. A yellow seat among the rest of the stadium's blue ones marks the spot where the ball landed. Boggs was inducted into the Baseball Hall of Fame in 2005, his first year of eligibility.

Chapter Five

Success on Ice Melts Floridians' Hearts

The Tampa Bay Lightning

Lightning Equality

Building a successful hockey franchise in Florida was a risk. Hockey is a winter sport. Before the game arrived in Florida, if you asked someone what first came to mind when they thought of hockey, they would most likely say things like ice, cold, winter, Canada. Before the arrival of the Tampa Bay Lightning, the southern-most U.S. team had been the Atlanta Flames, and they folded in 1980 and moved north to become the Calgary Flames. Selling the cold sport of hockey to the warmer climates of the southern states had proven difficult. The Los Angeles Kings had managed to survive in their market since breaking into the NHL in 1967, but attracting fans to the arena was a constant issue. They got a much-needed boost that probably saved their franchise when superstar Wayne Gretzky was acquired from the Edmonton Oilers before the 1988–89 season. All this to say that hockey is not a natural fit to southern states like Florida, and in order to get people's attention, a new franchise in the south needed something extra to pull people in.

When the NHL announced that it had awarded a new franchise to the city of Tampa, many were skeptical that the management team, led by Hall of Famers Phil and Tony Esposito, could bring in fans. Despite the questions surrounding the team's viability, players were chosen, coaches were hired and an arena was built to house the new Tampa Bay Lightning.

General manager Phil Esposito, a center who had played with Chicago, Boston and the New York Rangers, had been around the hockey and business world long enough to know that to get the public's attention, he needed something to lure them in. Prior to the start of the 1992–93 season, Esposito made headlines when he signed goaltender Manon Rhéaume to a professional contract. To have a female contracted to play on a professional hockey club got the media's attention in the Tampa Bay area and around the world.

Although many interpreted the move as a publicity stunt, Rhéaume was a serious hockey player who had proven herself in the past. She had already broken down barriers for women by being the first girl to play in the all-male International Pee Wee Hockey Tournament and had played one season (1991–92) with the Québec Major Junior Hockey League's Trois-Rivières Draveurs. She had all the necessary skills to be a top-quality goaltender and played the game just like any other player trying to make their way through the system. In addition to her skill set as a goaltender,

Rhéaume was hard working, approachable and very attractive. And despite the cries that her signing was merely a ploy to build interest in a team in a non-traditional market, throngs of media showed up at team practices, her face was plastered across every local Florida newspaper and the Canadian granted countless interviews before she had even stepped out onto the ice for a real NHL game.

A lot was said about her signing with the Lightning, both positive and negative, but Rhéaume managed to keep her focus on playing the game that she loved. If someone was willing to give her the opportunity to play in the NHL, regardless of their motives, she was going to take it.

"It's never been easy," Rhéaume said. "But I've always wanted to play hockey. I love hockey. I'd rather play hockey than do anything else. If you have that kind of desire, I think you can achieve what you want to achieve."

Her moment to prove to the world that she could hold her own against the NHL's best came in September 1992 in a preseason game against the St. Louis Blues. A crowd of more than 9000 took their seats before the start of the game to watch Rhéaume as she circled the rink and took a few shots during the warm-up. When the game finally started, she looked confident and managed to stop the first three shots that came her way. But her nerves finally got the better of her when she let in a long-range shot from the Blues' Jeff Brown. Then she let in another goal off Brendan Shanahan before the end of the first period. As the buzzer sounded for the first intermission, Rhéaume was given a warm round of applause for her effort. The French Canadian goaltender finished the historic moment with two goals allowed on nine shots. Not a bad accomplishment since the goaltender who replaced her for the remainder of the game, Wendell Young, allowed two goals as well.

Unfortunately, Rhéaume did not get to play in a regular season game. She was cut from the team shortly after her opening performance. She did make another preseason appearance for the Lightning against the Bruins in 1993, but again, she was taken out after one period. Publicity stunt or not, Manon Rhéaume and the Lightning had accomplished something that had never been done before. While it is not likely that an NHL team will ever have a permanent female player, Rhéaume took down the barrier and showed the world that women could play in a man's game. And all her hard work did pay off when she signed a three-year contract with the Lightning's farm team.

The Florida Panthers

The Rat Trick

The Detroit Red Wings have the tradition of throwing octopi onto the ice during the playoffs. The ritual honors their 1952 playoff run in which they won eight consecutive games to take the Stanley Cup. The long arms of the sea creature symbolize those eight wins, and octopi have been used ever since to bring the team good luck.

The Florida Panthers had been in the NHL for only two seasons, far too short a time to establish any lasting rituals, but at the beginning of the 1995–96 season, a strange animal appeared in the team's dressing room, sparking a tradition that continued all the way to the Stanley Cup finals.

The 1995–96 season was the Florida Panthers' third in the NHL, and like most new franchises in the league, their play on the ice was not of the highest caliber. Composed of the league's journeymen vets and rookies, the Panthers were tagged as highly likely to linger at the bottom of the league. This had been the way of the NHL since the 1967 expansion. New teams generally took a few years, if not more, to become competitive, and the Florida Panthers had already proven in their two previous seasons to be following that path. Sport often lends itself to superstition quite easily, and at the beginning of the 1995–96 season, an incident occurred that some might say gave the Panthers that extra little bit of luck they needed.

On October 8, as the team prepared for its home opener against the Calgary Flames, a rat suddenly appeared in the dressing room, scaring several players. Veteran tough guy Scott Mellanby stepped forward with his stick in hand and with full force, let fly a slap shot that sent the creature flying across the locker room, where it smashed into the concrete wall and was killed instantly.

"We were all dressed, ready to go on the ice for the first home game of the season," said Mellanby, a 29-year-old right winger. "The rat came into the room. Understandably, there was a lot of commotion. Everyone got pretty nervous and excited. I got nervous and excited. I guess I just reacted."

All the players had a good laugh about the incident and left the dressing room to play the game, not giving their dearly departed guest another thought as Mellanby scored two goals to help the team to a 4–3 win.

It was during the postgame media scrum that Panthers goaltender John Vanbiesbrouck mentioned the locker room incident and joked that while Mellanby failed to get a hat trick, he did manage to get a "rat trick." It was the perfect catchphrase for the media, and it hit the newsstands the next day. The team jokingly constructed a tiny memorial to the deceased rat, circling the exact spot of its demise on the wall with a felt-tipped pen and adding an inscription beneath that read "R.I.P. Rat 1."

The players quickly put the incident out of their minds as they focused on playing their next game. For the team, the story had ended, but the fans held onto the image of one of their Panthers taking out the weak rat, and at the next home game, when the Panthers scored, a fan threw a rubber rat onto the ice. At the next game, a few more rats hit the ice when the team scored, and then more rats after that in the next game. The Panthers began stringing together wins, and by the halfway mark of the season, they were one of the top five teams in the NHL. Their sudden rise in the standings had more to do with solid play on the ice, great coaching and a newfound sense of purpose, but fans fully embraced the superstitious power they believed to be behind the dead rat and kept tossing rubber rodents onto the ice every time the Panthers scored. The fans' suspicions of some sort of divine intervention were confirmed on February 19, 1996, when the Chinese calendar entered the Year of the Rat.

Most fans didn't care whether their team's success was the result of luck or hard work because the Panthers were winning, and by the end of the season, the team had made the playoffs for the first time. The playoff berth only increased the rat craze that had spread through the city of Miami and across South Florida. Rat fever set in as the Panthers beat the Boston Bruins and then the Philadelphia Flyers to reach the Eastern Conference finals against the Pittsburgh Penguins. Good old American capitalism took hold and local businesses cashed in on the frenzy. Supermarkets sold "rat cupcakes," and clothing stores and street vendors did a brisk business in rat-related T-shirts. The now-famous rubber rat became a hard commodity to find.

While the league and the team officially frowned on the practice of fans throwing things onto the ice during a game, Panthers management partnered with the Orkin pest-control company and hired a crew of 40-plus exterminators to clear the ice of rubber rats after each goal.

Against the Penguins, the rat tossing became a tsunami. During the seven-game series, as many as 3000 rats hit the ice after each Panthers goal. The luck of the rat continued to pay off as the team bested the Penguins in the seventh game and moved into the Stanley Cup finals against the Colorado Avalanche. For the first game of the series in Denver, Avalanche fans came prepared to show the Panthers just what they thought of their rubber rat tradition.

After the each of the three Colorado goals, fans littered the ice—with rat traps. The jinx worked, and the Avalanche won the first and second games on their home ice. Back in Miami for game three, Panthers fans did their best to prevent a premature end to the team's incredible season and had plenty of rats on hand. They were disappointed when the Avalanche's Claude Lemieux potted the first goal for a 1–0 lead. Later in the period, Panthers forward Ray Sheppard slipped the puck past goaltender Patrick Roy to tie the score at 1–1.

The instant the puck crossed the goal line, a barrage of rats poured down from the stands. During the season, goaltenders would normally take refuge in their nets during this ritual, but Roy stood defiantly out in the open. In just a few seconds, thousands and thousands of rubber, plastic and stuffed rats covered the ice. A similar scene unfolded minutes later when Rob Niedermayer scored to put the Panthers up 2–1 at the end of the first period. In the Avalanche dressing room, Roy stood up before his teammates and declared "No more rats!" Heeding their goaltender's words, the Penguins kept the Panthers scoreless for the rest of the game and won 3–2. Down three games to none, the Panthers needed a miracle to come back and win the Stanley Cup.

Backed into a corner in game four, instead of attacking, the Panthers played a strict defensive style.

The two teams played marathon scoreless hockey that lasted into the third overtime before Uwe Krupp scored an unassisted goal at the 4:31 mark, thus bringing an end to the Year of the Rat—on the ice.

The real rat at the beginning of the season had not died in vain, however, as the Panthers gave their fans something to believe in and helped to firmly root professional hockey in South Florida when most people thought it would fail. By giving up its life, albeit involuntarily, the rat had provided the young Panthers franchise and its fans with what they needed most—hope.

The league, though, did not think the rat craze of the 1995–96 season was good for the game, and as a direct result, it implemented a new rule prior to the 1996–97 season stating that if fans threw objects onto the ice, then the referee had the discretion to deliver a delay of game penalty to the home team. (There was, of course, an asterisk added to the paragraph that allowed the traditional tossing of hats onto the ice in the event of a hat trick.)

Richard Zednik's Close Call

Without a doubt, hockey is a dangerous sport. It is known as the fastest team sport in the world, and when combined with players the size of trees moving on solid ice on the edges of razor-sharp blades, accidents are bound to occur. The only player ever to die in an NHL game as the result of an injury was Minnesota North Star Bill Masterton, who suffered severe brain trauma after his helmet-less head smashed into the ice in a game on January 13, 1968.

One of the most gruesome injuries to occur in the NHL happened on March 22, 1989, to Buffalo Sabres goaltender Clint Malarchuk. During the game between the Sabres and the St. Louis Blues, two players were sent crashing into Malarchuk's net, and the skate of one of the players caught Malarchuk in the throat. In a matter of seconds, the ice was flooded with blood as Malarchuk tried to stop the flow from his neck. The skate had cut his internal carotid artery, leaving him with only minutes to live without medical assistance. Luckily, the trainers and doctors on staff managed to save his life, but the image of Malarchuk on his knees with blood pouring from his neck remains one of the most gruesome in hockey history.

Since that 1989 game, there had not been an injury of that magnitude in the NHL until February 10, 2008, in a game between the Florida Panthers and, coincidentally, the Buffalo Sabres. The incident occurred when Panthers forwards Olli Jokinen and Richard Zednik raced into the corner of the rink to get a loose puck, but Sabres forward Clarke MacArthur got in the way and Jokinen ended up tripping over his leg. As Jokinen flew through the air, his skate came up and caught Zednik in the throat, cutting open his external carotid artery. Blood immediately shot out of his neck, hitting the ice several feet in front of where he had been struck. Zednik skated to the Florida bench, leaving behind a trail of blood. He was taken to the dressing room, where doctors and trainers quickly dealt with the life-threatening injury.

"As soon as he got into the dressing room, I think they were able to stabilize him and stop the bleeding, which was probably crucial," said then–Panthers coach Jacques Martin at a postgame news conference.

Zednik was taken to hospital to undergo surgery, and a few days later, he was back home with his wife but was forced to miss the remainder the season. On February 20, Zednik gave his first press conference since the incident.

"I felt like somebody stabbed me. I knew exactly what happened, and I knew exactly what I had to do. I was like, 'Okay, this is it. I have to get up.' ...When I got to the bench, I knew it was an artery, the way the blood was going. I don't want to think about it, but I was in pretty bad shape."

Zednik was asked if he had seen the footage of the incident, and he replied that at first he did not want to see it, but then curiosity took over.

"At first when I was in the Buffalo hospital, I was like, 'No, I don't want to watch.' I was like, still kind of in shock. But then when I got back to Florida...I was curious, exactly, how the skate came to the neck," he said. "I watched it once. That's enough."

After seeing the injury on televison, former Sabres goaltender Clint Malarchuk tried to get a message to Zednik, but the Panthers right winger preferred not to discuss the incident and wanted to refocus on his career. Malarchuk had struggled with nightmares and flashbacks after his accident, and his career was never the same.

"I don't think it's something I want to talk about," Zednik said. "I want to focus on my career. I just think I'll be okay."

Chapter Six

Heat, Magic and King James

Skiles Sets the Table and Sets Record

By the time Scott Skiles was selected by the newly formed Orlando Magic in the 1989 NBA expansion draft, it was clear that the former All-American from Michigan State would not have as much impact in the pros as he did in college. This is not to say that Skiles was a bust—he just hadn't yet hit his stride in stops in Milwaukee and Indiana during his first three years in the NBA.

In 1990–91, his second season with the Magic, Skiles became the team's starting point guard. He averaged 17.2 points and 8.4 assists per game, and was named the league's Most Improved Player.

That same season also proved noteworthy in other ways for the former Indiana high school sensation. Before a hometown crowd at Orlando Arena on December 30, Skiles set a single-game record for assists, which still stands. On 30 occasions that night, he set up teammates to score in the Magic's 155–116 win over the Denver Nuggets.

"Double D" Made Opponents Pay

Just about everyone was expecting a record-setting career from Orlando native Darryl Dawkins when he jumped from high school straight to the Philadelphia 76ers. The six-foot, 11-inch center led Maynard Evans High School to a Florida state championship in 1975 and was the first prep player ever selected by an NBA team.

The Sixers were hoping that "Double D" would have an impact similar to that of Moses Malone, another high school phenom who bypassed college ball a year earlier when he joined the Utah Stars of the ABA.

It took a couple of seasons before Dawkins' raw talent developed and he began seeing substantial playing time. Although he was never an All-Star, Double D was a significant contributor as Philadelphia, led by Dr. J during that era, was a perennial playoff team that twice lost in the NBA finals.

The man known as "Chocolate Thunder" eventually made his mark by preventing opponents from scoring. But much to the chagrin of his coaches, not to mention NBA officials, it wasn't with great defense, but by fouling. Three times, Dawkins led the league in personal fouls. As a member of the New Jersey Nets in 1982–83, Dawkins committed a record 379 personal fouls. He then broke the record (which still stands) a year later as referees blew their whistles 386 times following his on-court transgressions.

This Hall of Fame hacker averaged at least four personal fouls per game for eight consecutive seasons, from 1979–80 to 1986–87, and finished his career with

2784 infractions in 726 games. That's a truly remarkable figure when placed alongside the great Wilt Chamberlain, who committed just 2075 fouls in 1045 games.

The Sun Shines on Mr. Mourning

By the end of the 1999–2000 season, Miami Heat center Alonzo Mourning had established himself as one of the best players in the NBA. The former Georgetown University standout was named to the All-Star team five times in his first eight seasons, and he had just copped his second consecutive Defensive Player of the Year award.

However, prior the start of the 2000–01 season, Mourning was diagnosed with focal segmental glomerulosclerosis, a kidney disease that attacks the tiny filters in the organ responsible for removing waste from the blood. This makes the kidney spill protein into the urine. The resulting damage can lead to kidney failure, which requires dialysis or a transplant.

The ailment had caused Mourning to miss all but 13 games that season. He returned for the 2001–02 campaign, but missed the entire next season and was eventually released by Miami. Mourning played briefly with the New Jersey Nets, but his health deteriorated, and he retired in November 2004 when his doctors told him that it was no longer medically safe for him to play basketball. A month later, Mourning underwent a successful kidney transplant. He received the new organ from a cousin, Jason Cooper, whom he had not seen in 25 years.

After recuperating, "Zo" rejoined the Nets but was traded to the Toronto Raptors, for whom he never played a game, and he subsequently rejoined the Heat in 2005. Mourning never again played at the level that made him an elite player, but he did play in 65 games in 2005–06, averaging 7.8 points and 5.5 rebounds per game as the Heat won its first and only NBA championship. He played two more seasons before retiring for good in 2009.

Mourning received many honors for a career well played and a life well lived. Along with his wife, Tracy, he has been active in several "youth focus" charities ever since he moved to the Miami area. The Heat recognized their all-time leading scorer with a special night in his honor and by retiring his number 33 jersey. In 2009, he received a further honor when a new local high school was named the Alonzo and Tracy Mourning Senior High Biscayne Bay Campus.

The Lebron James Story

After the retirement of Michael Jordan, the NBA suffered from the lack of a real, transformative superstar. Sure, there were the likes of Shaquille O'Neal and Kobe Bryant, but they had failed to cross that divide and enter mainstream culture. But then along came the savior, Lebron Raymone James, from Akron, Ohio. Even before he set foot in the professional ranks and proved himself, he had already been anointed as "the next great thing" while playing for his high school basketball team. Many teams would have given up a few of their best players just to get their hands on the number one pick overall at the 2003 NBA draft when James became eligible, but that opportunity fell directly in the lap of the Cleveland Cavaliers. Managers must have offered the Cavaliers a slew of players and cash in return for that selection, but they knew what they had and signed the young protégé to a long-term contract with his free agent rights coming up at the end of the 2009–10 season.

Time passed and Lebron James definitely lived up to expectations. The Cavaliers went from being one of the worst teams in the league to real contenders for the championship in just a few years. James saved the franchise from extinction and brought a level of celebrity to the working-class city. It was the perfect place for the Ohio native to begin his career, but other teams sat quietly on the sidelines, waiting for the end of the 2009–10 season, when James officially became a free agent.

Then it happened. At 12:01 AM eastern standard time on July 1, 2010, Lebron James officially entered free agency, meaning he could choose to play for any team he wanted. Since he had declined to sign a contract extension with the Cavaliers, speculation as to where the superstar would land started long before the end of the 2009–10 season. In order to lure James away from Cleveland, several cities began major campaigns to woo "the King" to their city.

To understand the hysteria surrounding James' free agency for those who may be unfamiliar with the ins and outs of professional basketball, you must first understand what it means to have a player like Lebron

James in your city. Players such as Michael Jordan in basketball and Wayne Gretzky in hockey are more than simply great players in their respective sports. They are a select few who have broken free of the bonds of their sport and managed to grab the attention of a wider audience, bringing with them attention to the sport and the team, and the money that inevitably follows.

Like it or not, Lebron James is more than just a man—he is a brand, and as such, a lot of money rides on where he plays, what type of shoes he wears, what car he drives and what restaurants he visits. Marquee players like James bring their notoriety and fame to any city in which they play, and people will spend money to be within the glow of that brand. In the case of Lebron James, his brand represents the potential of billions of dollars to the cities and companies that follow his every move.

James and all those around him are aware of that fact, making James a highly sought-after commodity. During the 2009–10 NBA season, the largest question that hung over the league was where Lebron James would sign when he became a free agent. Teams around the league had begun courting campaigns in order to entice him into signing with their NBA franchise. The city of New York was not shy about its desire to lure James out of Cleveland, and Cleveland worked equally hard to try to keep their star athlete. Throughout the entire process, James remained stoically silent about his choice. After the end of the 2009–10 season, the speculation ramped up when James' friend Chris

Bosh moved from the Toronto Raptors to the Miami Heat and another good friend, Dwayne Wade, signed a contract extension furthering his play in Miami for years into the future.

New York still hoped that "King James" would come to the Big Apple as it would be the perfect venue to showcase the Lebron James brand, and the Knicks were willing to shell out the big dollars. It would be the equivalent of Michael Jordan leaving the Chicago Bulls before the dynasty era. Cleveland still held hopes that James would choose to stay in his home state, but as the countdown to decision day loomed ever closer, it began to look more like the Miami Heat were to be the recipients of King James' graces.

Leading up to the decision, James' every move was scrutinized, and even the celebrity gossip website TMZ.com got into the mix, reporting on what city James was in on a given day and with whom he was having lunch. Then James announced that on July 8, 2010, he would give an hour-long interview to ESPN and reveal to the world who had won the King James sweepstakes. Never before in the history of sports had one player's free agency caused such an uproar. Parties formed across the nation as millions of basketball fans tuned in to ESPN and saw James take a seat in front of interviewer Jim Gray. In the first few moments of the interview, Lebron James finally revealed his secret. Fans in Cleveland held their breath as the words began to flow out of James' mouth through the television and into their ears, "This fall I am…" (everything is okay so far) "taking my talents to..." (here it comes, he is about to reveal his decision) "South Beach and play with the Miami Heat. The major factor was the best opportunity for me to win, to win now and for the future, also. Winning is the most important thing for me. I feel like this is going to be the best opportunity."

While boardrooms and bars across South Florida erupted with glee, back in Cleveland, the mood was much less joyous. James had taken the breath out of the entire city. The day after his decision, stocks for the Cleveland Cavaliers franchise plummeted in the markets, while those of companies associated with the Miami Heat soared. Season tickets on the open market jumped in value by several thousand dollars in Miami as people clamored to get their first glimpse of their new hero. (Tickets prices in the cities he *could* have ended up in rose a little prior to his announcement.) It was party time in Miami as business owners and merchants throughout the city began their preparations for the King's arrival.

In Cleveland, the mood was a lot less festive. Miami's gain was Cleveland's loss. Fans took the dramatic way in which he announced his decision as a slap in the face. Instantly, Lebron James jerseys were removed from stores and a huge, five-story billboard of the star player was removed from the center of Cleveland. The next day, Cavs owner Dan Gilbert published an open letter to fans that did not shy away from criticism. Below is just a small sampling:

"As you know, our former hero, who grew up in the very region that he deserted this evening, is no longer a Cleveland Cavalier. This was announced with a several-day, narcissistic, self-promotional buildup culminating with a national TV special of his 'decision' unlike anything ever witnessed in the history of sports...

I PERSONALLY GUARANTEE THAT THE CLEVELAND CAVALIERS WILL WIN AN NBA CHAMPIONSHIP BEFORE THE SELF-TITLED FORMER 'KING' WINS ONE.

You can take it to the bank."

Now part of the Miami Heat, James handed over his lucky number 23 jersey and took on a new identity as number 6. In the 2010–11 season, Lebron James will join Chris Bosch, Dwayne Wade and a host of other talented athletes on one of the teams slated to challenge for the NBA title. James has been anointed the new King of Miami, but if he cannot deliver a championship, then one wonders how long Heat fans will allow him to keep his throne.

Chapter Seven

The Net, the Ring, the Ponies and the Superstars

Tennis

Hart Had Heart

Born on June 20, 1925, in St. Louis, Missouri, Doris Hart began collecting Grand Slam titles while she was still an undergraduate at the University of Miami. But the career of one of the sporting world's greatest champions almost never occurred. As a child, Hart contracted osteomyelitis, an infection of the bone and bone marrow, the same disease that nearly ended the career—before it began—of New York Yankee great Mickey Mantle.

Some doctors recommended amputation, but Hart's parents refused. Instead, she underwent physical therapy, which included learning to play tennis. Her passion for the game increased, and she excelled on the court despite a permanently impaired right leg.

By age 16, she was nationally ranked in the top 10 and remained among the sport's elite players until her retirement in 1955, after she won the U.S. Championship singles title. Her first Grand Slam title was in women's doubles at Wimbledon in 1947. Hart, who made the Coral Gables area of Miami her home, added her first Grand Slam singles title two years later at the Australian Open.

Hart had a great on-court rivalry with Maureen Connolly, the teen sensation of the late 1940s and early 1950s. In 1953, the 18-year-old Connelly became the first woman, and only the second player, to win all four Grand Slam singles championships in the same year. Hart was her victim at the French Open, Wimbledon and the U.S. Open.

One of only two women to have defeated Connolly in a Grand Slam singles tournament, Hart won their second round match at the 1950 U.S. Championships, 6–2, 7–5. (Barbara Scofield, who defeated Connolly in the second round of the 1949 U.S. Championships, 6–4, 6–3, is the other.) Until then, Connolly had a perfect 9–0 record in Grand Slam singles finals, having defeated Hart in the final of four of them.

By the time she retired at age 30, Hart had captured 35 Grand Slam titles, tying her for fifth on the all-time list—which includes men—with Brough Clapp. Ahead of Hart are Margaret Osborne duPont (37), Billie Jean King (39), Martina Navratilova (59) and Margaret Court (62). Six of Hart's titles were in women's singles, 14 in women's doubles and 15 in mixed doubles. This includes a remarkable streak in which Hart won all 13 of the Grand Slam mixed doubles tournaments she played, beginning with the 1951 French Championships and extending through the 1955 U.S. Championships. During this period, she won five Wimbledon Championships, three French Championships and five U.S. Championships.

Hart also joins Court and Navratilova as one of the only players to win the "boxed set" of championships: singles, same-sex doubles and mixed doubles from all four Grand Slam events.

Hart Hits the Trifecta

Hart's third trip to the finals at Wimbledon came on July 7, 1951. She easily beat her good friend Shirley Fry in the finals, 6–1, 6–0, in one of the quickest matches in history, lasting only 36 minutes. But Hart was not done. Later in the day, she teamed with Fry to win the women's doubles crown, beating defending champions Louise Brough and Margaret Osborne duPont, 6–3, 13–11. Hart then capped her career day by pairing with her mixed doubles partner, Frank Segmen of Australia, to beat Mervyn Rose and Nancye Bolton, 7–5, 6–2, in that final.

Royal Exchange

You won't find Gardnar Mulloy at the top of any historical Grand Slam tennis rankings, but he was known to tennis fans who followed the sport in the 1950s. The brash, handsome player won five Grand Slam doubles events during the 1940s and '50s. Although "Gar" was a nationally ranked singles player, he did his best work with partners. He eventually became the tennis coach at the University of Miami, the school from which he had graduated in 1936.

Mulloy, who was born in Washington, DC, but grew up in Miami, partnered with Bill Talbert to capture the U.S. Championship in 1942, 1945, 1946 and 1948. And in 1957, at age 46 years and 226 days, Mulloy became the oldest man to win a Wimbledon title when he partnered with Budge Patty to take the men's doubles.

When promoting his autobiography in the spring of 2010, the 96-year-old Mulloy, who played competitively on senior circuits until 2006, said that despite winning the doubles title at Wimbledon, it was an event that began off the court that was the most memorable.

At a garden party thrown years earlier during the Wimbledon fortnight, Mulloy met Crown Princess Elizabeth, the oldest daughter and heir to the throne of Britain's King George VI. Mulloy asked the princess why she hadn't attended the tournament that year.

When informed by a defensive party hostess that Elizabeth's official duties precluded her from attending tennis matches, Mulloy flirtatiously replied, "I thought perhaps you weren't able to get tickets, which I would be happy to provide."

In 1957, Mulloy, by now age 43, won his only Wimbledon Championship with Patty. Making the presentation to the winners on Centre Court that year was Queen Elizabeth II, in her first trip to the tournament since becoming queen four years earlier.

After bowing and receiving the Wimbledon Championship Cup from the queen, Mulloy asked her if she remembered him.

"Yes, Mr. Mulloy," she replied. "I remember you quite well. As a matter of fact, I had difficulty getting in today, as you forgot to leave me tickets."

Game, set, match!

Boxing

The Dundees Bring Big-time Boxing to Florida

Boxing, along with baseball and horse racing, was a major professional sport in pre–World War II America. Boxing matches had been staged in Florida for decades, but not on a championship level. Nearly all major world championship bouts took place in New York and other large northern cities.

That all changed when Chris Dundee moved his promotional business from New York to Miami in 1950. Dundee, whose real name was Cristofo Mirena, entered the boxing world in New York in 1932, but he didn't manage his first world champion until he guided middleweight Ken Overlin to the title in 1940. The young Mirena changed his name to keep his parents from knowing that he was involved in the sport. His younger brother, Angelo, would later follow the new family "tradition" of changing his name to Dundee.

Chris Dundee, who had mild success up north, staked a claim in South Florida as boxing began to diversify in the early 1950s, thanks in large part to a new household item called television.

Dundee would put on shows at his own venue, the Miami Beach Auditorium, and he purchased the vacant space above a liquor store and converted it into a gym. He convinced Angelo to leave New York and run the "new" gym for him. Once the necessary renovations were completed, it was given the name the Fifth Street Gym.

It wasn't long before the Dundees had an impressive stable of young talent. Chris sometimes promoted shows several times a month and eventually staged eight world championship events, including the first Ali vs. Liston fight in 1964.

Over the next 35 years, many of boxing's greatest champions fought on Dundee's cards and trained at the gym. It was a magnet for exiled Cuban fighters in the late 1950s and early '60s as they fled Castro's communist regime.

Boxing fans who lived in the area or who traveled to Florida on vacation knew where to head to see some of the top fighters train. Young Cassius Clay, who later changed his name to Muhammad Ali, relocated to Miami shortly after turning pro to train under Angelo Dundee. Throughout the years, the gym also housed other famous champions such as Roberto Duran, Kid Gavilan, Luis Rodriguez and Alexis Arguello.

Using the gym as a base of operations and his older brother's considerable influence, Angelo became one of the top trainers in the sport. From his first world champion, Carmen Basilio in the 1950s, through Ali and culminating with George Foreman's miracle knockout win in 1994, Angelo worked the corners of 15 world champions.

Now based in the Tampa area, Angelo continues to train boxers. Chris Dundee lived in Miami until his death in 1998 at age 90. Both men are enshrined in the International Boxing Hall of Fame in Canasota, New York.

Ferdie Pacheco: The Fight Doctor

Ferdie Pacheco is one of Florida's great renaissance men. He has been a licensed pharmacist and a doctor, as well as a boxing cornerman, boxing analyst, novelist, screenwriter and artist. His paintings and drawings have been showcased around the world. Pacheco has received numerous awards for his artistic talent as well as Emmy Awards for his work in television as a commentator, producer and writer.

The Ybor City native first gained recognition in the sporting world in the early 1960s as "the Fight Doctor" because he was a licensed physician and a cornerman for the legendary heavyweight champion, Muhammad Ali. Pacheco, who earned a bachelor's degree from the University of Florida and a medical degree from the University of Miami, set up a practice in the Little Havana section of Miami in the late 1950s. Some of his patients were recently exiled boxers from Castro's Cuba, as well as other Central and South American fighters, many of whom plied their trade at Miami's historic Fifth Street Gym. Two major players at the gym in this era, known as Miami's "Golden Age" of boxing, were Chris and Angelo Dundee.

Pacheco treated many of Angelo Dundee's fighters and eventually worked the corner of 12 world champions. He was part of what he called "the Ali Circus" and was in the Greatest's corner for all his major fights, including all three epic bouts with Joe Frazier, three battles with Ken Norton and the historic "Rumble in the Jungle" against George Foreman.

It was Pacheco who first noticed Ali's diminishing physical skills and urged the three-time heavyweight champion to retire. Ali ignored his doctor's advice, and soon after, Pacheco left his camp.

In the mid-1970s, Pacheco switched to television commentary, and over the next 20 years, he was a regular at ringside for CBS, NBC, Showtime and Univision. He continues to paint—his work is on permanent display in the state capitol in Tallahassee—and he has authored several books on boxing, art and cooking. The lifelong resident of Florida, now in his 80s, still resides in Miami.

A Writer's Best Friend

In the pre-Internet age, it often proved difficult for boxing writers to get research material for feature stories. If a writer couldn't find the information in a book at the local library or in the *New York Times* microfilm, he only had one other option—to call Hank Kaplan in Miami. Luckily, that living, breathing resource had an internationally recognized reputation for reliability.

Kaplan, the former publisher of *International Boxing Digest* in the 1970s, had perhaps the largest private collection in the world of boxing books, photographs and newspaper and magazine clippings. His house was a virtual boxing library, and his ability to recall names, fight results and other historical facts made the self-described "boxing archivist" the go-to man for boxing writers, as well as book publishers and television producers.

Kaplan's well-earned reputation as a boxing historian earned him a position on the International Boxing Hall of Fame's screening committee, a position he held from the hall's inception in 1989 until his death in 2007.

The quotable Brooklyn, New York, native, who moved to South Florida after World War II, was also used as an expert consultant by ESPN, HBO, Showtime and many other media outlets worldwide. In his travels to world title fights around the globe, Kaplan would often look up and visit the descendants and living relatives of legendary boxers. More information gathered and more stories to tell.

In 2002, the Boxing Writers Association of America honored Kaplan with the James J. Walker Award for long and meritorious service to boxing. His unselfish contributions to the sport were further acknowledged in 2006, when he was inducted into the International Boxing Hall of Fame's "Observer" category, which is reserved for media and other individuals who make significant contributions to the squared circle.

The Lip Silences the Bear

If there was ever a professional athlete who deserved to be feared, it was Charles "Sonny" Liston. He was from the "other" side of the tracks, had a criminal record, served time in prison for armed robbery and could knock men out with a single punch with either hand. He did this for a living inside, and at times outside, the boxing ring. And by the time he was a serious contender for the heavyweight championship, he had the backing of the syndicate—the mob.

Beginning in 1958, Liston began the first of his seven trips to Miami to box at Chris Dundee's Miami Auditorium. The first six were as a contender; the seventh and final time was as the heavyweight champion of the world.

Never, as in *never* before had a heavyweight champion been looked at with contempt. Sure, most fighters are from poor backgrounds, but few with a criminal record had become champion. Perhaps Liston's quiet, shy persona had something to do with the fact that he was illiterate. So he simply kept quiet—and let his fists do the talking.

After winning the heavyweight title from Floyd Patterson in September 1962 with a brutal first-round knockout, Liston duplicated the feat, stopping the former champ again in round one of their July 1963 rematch. Liston's destruction of Patterson added significantly to his already forbidding reputation. Next in line to challenge him was a brash, bigmouthed kid from Louisville, Kentucky, named Cassius Clay.

Few boxing fans gave the bombastic 22-year-old Clay a realistic chance of defeating Liston. Although Clay was undefeated in 19 prior fights, he had never beaten a fighter with Liston's record or reputation and was perceived to be a flake by most of the boxing press. Nobody was surprised when Liston was installed as an 8-to-1 betting favorite.

The so-called experts failed to recognize that Liston, whose birth certificate said he was just a few months shy of his 32nd birthday (most people believed he was at least five years older), had only boxed a total of six rounds in his four one-sided bouts since 1960. Ring rust, not to mention Father Time, would play a factor against a younger, quicker and, something nobody seemed to acknowledge, bigger challenger.

Clay won the gold medal at the 1960 Rome Olympics as a light heavyweight. He had grown since then and now stood six feet, three inches tall and had filled out to a lean 210 pounds. In comparison, Liston was a rock-solid six feet, one inch and 218 pounds.

Few boxing fans expected a competitive fight, perhaps explaining why only 8200 spectators were on hand on February 25, 1964, at Convention Hall in Miami Beach, which had a capacity of 15,000. A cold, confident Liston charged from his corner at the opening bell, but he was unable to catch his fleet-footed challenger.

Clay scored throughout the early rounds with crisp jabs to the champion's face mixed in with an occasional combination. By the end of the third round, it was evident that the young boxer's punches were scoring—Liston had a mouse under his right eye and a cut under his left. Clay was winning the fight.

After round four, Clay came back to the corner in a panic, saying he couldn't see because something was in his eyes. It was later determined that a substance likely used to treat Liston's cuts had unintentionally gotten on his gloves and then into Clay's eyes.

Clay told Angelo Dundee, his cornerman, to cut off his gloves—he didn't want to continue. But Dundee quickly restored calm. He flushed his charge's eyes with a water-filled sponge and then sent him out for round five with instructions to dance.

Former champion Joe Louis, who was an expert commentator on the television broadcast, noticed the commotion in the challenger's corner and dutifully noted that there was a problem with Clay's eyes.

For the first half of the fifth round, Liston had a little success connecting with the nearly blind Clay. But around the halfway point of the round, the fighting Kentuckian regained his sight and held his own the rest of the way. Liston had missed his chance.

Speed kills, but first it frustrates. A half hour earlier, Liston had seemed indestructible. Now, with his opponent scoring at will, Liston appeared timid—he was an emperor without clothes. As Clay's punches continued to land on the champion's face, former champ Louis remarked that the youngster was gaining confidence and that Liston's reign as champion was indeed in peril.

Clay continued to score as his opponent's punches found mostly air. The soon-to-be ex-champion could not get out of the way of the punches from his younger, quicker foe.

Between rounds, Liston's corner tried to work on the cuts under his eyes, but it was clear that something was wrong. Clay was on his feet eagerly awaiting the bell for round seven, but it was not to be. Claiming an injury to his left shoulder, Liston quit on his stool.

The new champion danced in the middle of the ring and proclaimed, "I'm king of the world!...I'm a baaaad man!"

And the new king of the boxing world wasn't finished issuing proclamations. Next he announced that he had become a Muslim and changed his name. He would go on to fight all over the world as Muhammad Ali.

A Surreal Reel Event

Although Muhammad Ali never again fought in Miami Beach, he did have a memorable encounter there with former champ Rocky Marciano in the fall of 1969. Before the invention of PlayStation and EA Sports video games, the outcomes of historical matchups between boxing champions were the source of endless debate.

But in 1969, a radio executive named Murray Woroner launched a "computerized" boxing tournament that featured the 16 greatest heavyweight champions of all time. However, the tournament lost credibility when it had Ali losing to Jim Jeffries, who reigned from 1899 to 1904. How was it possible for Jeffries, who had been soundly beaten in real life by superior boxer Jack Johnson, to beat Ali? Ali was not only bigger than both Jeffries and Johnson but was also regarded as the fastest heavyweight in history.

At this time, Ali was no longer the heavyweight champion. He had been stripped of the title and had his boxing license revoked in 1967 when he refused to be inducted into the U.S. Army. The self-proclaimed "Greatest of All Times" not only questioned the outcome of his computerized "fight" with the deceased former champ, but he also filed a lawsuit against Woroner for defamation of character. A settlement was reached when Woroner proposed another computerized bout that would feature Ali against Rocky Marciano. Only this fight would not be held on radio; it would appear on movie screens in the U.S., Canada and Great Britain.

Marciano had retired with a record of 49–0 after his knockout of Archie Moore in 1955. The former champ, now age 46, went into training, dropped nearly 50 pounds and wore a toupee to conceal his balding head. The fight would be staged without a crowd at a Miami television studio with local promoter Chris Dundee serving as the referee.

Ali, who was also undefeated, would have his trusted cornerman Angelo Dundee at his side. Both men would be paid approximately $10,000 plus a percentage of the gate from the approximately 1500 theaters and arenas that were scheduled to show the event on closed-circuit television.

What Woroner tried to do was proffer an outcome that boxing fans might not agree with, but would acknowledge was at least plausible. The two principals met at the television studio and filmed a total of 70 largely choreographed, one-minute rounds, based on data supplied from Woroner's computer. It was agreed that head punches would be pulled, but body blows were fair game. For the broadcast, former heavyweight champs Jim Braddock, Joe Louis, Max Schmeling,

Jack Sharkey and Jersey Joe Walcott provided analysis and commentary.

What fans saw was the exiled Ali out-box the slower Marciano in the early going. While Marciano worked Ali's body, the eventual three-time champ opened up cuts over both of Marciano's eyes. This was an injury that several of Mariano's opponents had inflicted in the past.

As the bout progressed into the later rounds, the Brockton Blockbuster's body attack started to take its toll on Ali. Marciano was knocked down for a short count in round eight, but he stuck to a game plan that had served him well so many times in the past and knocked Ali down late in the 10th round. The momentum had changed for good, and Marciano sealed the deal with a left hook that sent Ali to the canvas for a 10-count late in round 13.

Unfortunately, Marciano died three weeks after shooting wrapped. Woroner's computer had the popular, undefeated Marciano stopping Ali in round 13. However, boxing fans in England saw a different outcome—Ali stopping the Brockton Blockbuster on cuts late in the fight.

It's worth noting that Woroner's fantasy matchup generated a live closed-circuit gate of approximately $5 million.

Hitting Bottom at the Orange Bowl

It was not unusual for two-time world champion Roberto Duran to hear the crowd roaring as he sat in his dressing room waiting to get the call to head to the ring. By 1982, he had been one of boxing's marquee attractions for 10 years.

The famed "Manos de Piedra" (Hands of Stone) from Panama had been the main event in all four of his prior fights in South Florida, two of which were defenses of his world lightweight title. But the setting at the Orange Bowl on the night of November 12, 1982, was one he hadn't experienced in a long time. Although the cheers from the crowd concerned the action in the main event, Duran was not on the mind of any of the 30,000 fans in attendance.

He waited in his dressing room and watched on closed-circuit television what everyone else at the Orange Bowl and millions around the world were enjoying on television—the epic first fight between International Boxing Federation (IBF) junior welterweight champion Aaron Pryor and Alexis Arguello.

It was just a few weeks shy of the second anniversary of Duran's shocking surrender to Sugar Ray Leonard in their New Orleans rematch. Until that fateful night, the Panamanian had been regarded as the best—and most feared—boxer in the world. But now Duran's stock was in free fall. After quitting against Leonard, he won two tune-up bouts before dropping a one-sided, unanimous decision to Wilfred Benitez in January 1982. Later that September in Detroit, Duran was upset by an unknown journeyman named Kirkland Laing of Britain.

Now, abandoned by his longtime trainers and manager, as well as his promoter, Don King, Duran went to the ring on the "walk out" bout while the media went to the postfight press conference to interview the main event participants and the crowd of 30,000 headed to postfight parties in South Beach.

Against journeyman Jimmy Batten, another Brit, Duran labored to a unanimous decision witnessed by those whose chief concern was avoiding a traffic jam. Early accounts of the Pryor vs. Arguello fight card failed to mention the Duran vs. Batten contest, since the fight took place after the scribes had filed their stories for their first editions.

It was just as well for Duran, who was the only person who still believed that he had anything left. Surprisingly, it turned out that he did. Two and a half months later, he was back in the main event, although as an underdog, against house favorite Jose "Pipino" Cuevas, who he stopped in four rounds in Los Angeles. In his next fight, against World Boxing Association (WBA) junior middleweight champion Davey Moore, Duran thrilled a sellout crowd at Madison Square Garden with an eighth-round knockout to become just the seventh man in boxing history to win world championships in three different weight divisions.

Horse Racing

Legendary Citation's Tragic Change in Jockeys

Horse racing fans were expecting a banner year from Citation in 1948. As a two-year-old, the promising thoroughbred, ridden by jockey Al Snider, won eight of his nine starts and was named the best two-year-old in 1947. Citation's campaign as a three-year-old started where the previous one left off. He won the Seminole Handicap, then the Everglades Stakes and the Flamingo Stakes at Hialeah Park in Miami.

Shortly after those wins, Snider went fishing off the Florida Keys, and his small boat got caught in a storm. He drowned, and his body was never recovered. Citation's trainers replaced Snider with one of the jockey's friends, Eddie Arcaro. In the first start after Snider's death, Citation placed second in the Chesapeake Trial Stakes, but it was the last race the horse lost that year.

Arcaro guided Citation to 15 consecutive wins, including the Kentucky Derby, Preakness Stakes and Belmont Stakes, making him only the eighth horse in history to win the Triple Crown. The jockey gave a portion of his Kentucky Derby purse to Snider's widow.

Citation ran his last race in 1951 and retired with a record of 32 wins, 10 shows and two place finishes in 45 starts. He finished out of the money just once and was the first horse to earn more than $1 million.

Shoe's Last Trip to the Winner's Circle

Legendary jockey Willie Shoemaker made his reputation by riding winners on thoroughbred racing tracks from the East Coast to the West Coast and all points in between. The Fabens, Texas, native, who stood just four feet, 11 inches tall and weighed 95 pounds, turned pro in 1949 at age 17. In a career that spanned 41 years, "The Shoe" won more races than any jockey in history.

Shoemaker finished as the top-earning jockey of the year 10 times, and he led all jockeys in wins five times. His mounts finished first in 11 Triple Crown races: the Kentucky Derby (4), the Preakness Stakes (2) and the Belmont Stakes (5). He also had one Breeders Cup win, which came in 1987.

The man who once said, "There are one hundred and ninety nine ways to get beat, but only one way to win: get there first," did that for the last of his then-record 8839 winning rides on January 20, 1990, at Gulfstream Park. Shoemaker guided Beau Genius to victory in the Hallandale Handicap, thus earning his last trip to the winner's circle. He retired two weeks later after his 40,350th race, at age 58, as the winningest jockey of all time. Shoemaker's career win total has since been eclipsed by Panama-born Laffit Pincay Jr., with 9530 wins, who passed Shoemaker in 1999, and Canadian Russell Baze, who won his 11,000 race in August 2010.

Golf

Heartless Golfers

In 1992, 65-year-old Donald DeGreve was golfing near his home in Winter Haven when he felt a sharp pain in his chest. He keeled over on the 16th green and died. But it was league day at the club, and dozens of golfers needed to play through, so instead of taking DeGreve's body off the course, someone simply placed a white sheet over the corpse. Dozens of golfers passed his body laid out on the 16th green all day long, avoiding any contact with poor Donald while club management tried to find his wife so that she could retrieve the body. One of the golfers reportedly said, rather coldly, "Life goes on, so we had to keep going." Ouch.

Jai Alai

Basque Ball

Nestled between the snowy peaks of the Pyrenees Mountains and Southern France is a little area of the world that's home to a distinct people who, although they live within the geographic borders of Spain, refer to themselves as the Basque. It was during the Middle Ages, around the 13th century, that a type of handball game first appeared in this area. Known at first simply as *pelota*, the men of the villages played this handball game at festivals. Later, a new name came into use for the sport, *jai alai*, which simply means "happy festival." Although jai alai is a Basque term and the game was created in the Basque region, the Basque do not use the name jai alai, preferring to use *pelota vasca* (Basque ball). It's equivalent to North Americans using the word "soccer" to refer to the game that the rest of the world calls football. (For the linguists, "soccer" is actually a word of British origin and not an American creation, as many believe.)

Jai alai is one of the fastest sports on the planet, with the ball traveling at top speeds of over 180 miles per hour. The playing area is a rectangular court, 176 feet long by 40 feet wide, consisting of three walls (front, back and left) and the floor, which is also in play. The right wall (usually a very large, glass partition to allow viewing) is considered out of play. The playing area is delineated by a series of lines marking the boundaries of the court. There are typically two teams of two players on the court at one time. Each team consists of a frontcourt and a backcourt player, and the game begins when the frontcourt player serves the ball to the second team, as in tennis. But unlike tennis, in which two players or teams play against the same opponents for an entire game, in jai alai, the winner of the point gets to stay on the court to meet the next team in the rotation. Losers go to the end of the line to wait for their return to the court. The first team to score seven points wins the match.

Some sports historians suggest that the element of bouncing the ball off a wall was first introduced into the game during the 15th century. According to this theory, the soldiers of the infamous Spanish conquistador Hernán Cortés took that feature of the game from a similar Aztec handball game and introduced it into the game played in Spain. The new addition to the sport spread across the country and became especially prominent in the Basque region.

Sport Embodies Culture

At first, jai alai sounds like a simple game played by children, but the sport that developed out of the Basque region embodied many of the values of traditional Basque life, in which the daily struggles were hard and required much strength and courage. The key element of the game in which a player strikes a very hard ball with a bare hand speaks to this courage and strength.

Every player who participated in the sport knew that tolerating the pain better than your opponent was a sign of virtue and courage. Though the game was relatively simple—make your opponent miss the ball and you gain a point—successful players had to be strong and agile. The truly skillful had a well of stamina and consistency that would last throughout a match. It was this cultural need to test one's physical strength and stamina that the Basque carried with them when they migrated to the New World.

New World Innovations

Although the foundations of the game developed in the Old World, jai alai as it is played today would not have been possible without input from the New World. Up until the 19th century, the speed of the ball was limited because of the materials used in its construction, and the sport was still played with bare hands. In the 19th century, a new substance called rubber was used in manufacturing the jai alai ball, making it a lot livelier. It is impossible to say whether the first rubber ball was created in the Americas or in Europe, but without the raw material from the rubber tree, the evolution of the game would have halted.

By the time the rubber ball was introduced, the Basque handball game had spread throughout the Americas. As the speed of the game increased, many players incurred injuries, mostly of the broken hand sort. It was this type of injury that Argentinean pelota player Melchor Guruceaga was recovering from when he came up with a design that would forever change the sport. Unable to play his favorite game because of a broken wrist, Guruceaga developed a long, scoop-like, wicker basket that he attached to his injured hand. It made it easier to catch the ball and provided protection for the catching hand. The design caught on and spread through the Americas and back to Europe.

Jai Alai in Florida

Although jai alai technically originated in the Basque region of Spain, it has been the players in the Americas who have truly embraced the sport, and its most prominent center today is in South Florida.

By the early 20th century, jai alai had become very popular in many Latin American countries, most notably Mexico and Cuba. The United States got its first real taste of the game during the 1904 Summer Olympics in St. Louis, when jai alai was played as one of the exhibition sports. The popularity of the game increased, and, in 1924, it was introduced as a tourist attraction in Miami. But one of the biggest factors responsible for the spread of the sport came in two waves. In 1936, it became legal to bet on the outcome of games, and in 1959, when Fidel Castro took power in Cuba, a wave of immigrants to the shores of the Sunshine State brought new life to the jai alai communities in South Florida. To this day, there are more jai alai frontons in Florida than in any other region of the world. Florida has become the unofficial home of North American–style jai alai and is one of the major destinations for professional players.

Jai alai is not like other typical professional sports with proper leagues, teams and team rivalries. Although there are people who take to the sport for the love of the game, many are more interested in the specific outcome of each game for betting purposes.

A Brief Jai Alai Glossary

Aja: The red, fringed sash worn as part of the standard uniform of white shoes and trousers and the colored and numbered shirts indicating post positions

Bote pronto: A ball that is picked up off the court floor on a short hop; one of the most difficult catches in jai alai

Fronton: The open-walled court where the sport is played, which consists of three walls (front, left and back); the right wall is clear glass to allow spectators to view the game safely

Cesta: The basket attached to the player's hand that is used to catch the ball

Cesta punta: Literally "basket" and "tip"; the Spanish name for the sport of jai alai

Pelota: The ball used in the game

Pelotaria: A jai alai player; from the Spanish *pelota* (and the French *pelote*), meaning "ball"

Picada: A throw tossed straight overhand with a quick turn of the wrist, resulting in a high bounce

Remate: A move in which a ball thrown from the left side caroms off two walls; commonly thought of as the most effective way to win a point

Rebote: Returning the pelota from the back wall with a forehand or backhand shot

The Superstars

The Best of the Best

One of the most contentious debates among sports aficionados is: Who is the best athlete in the world? Does he or she play football, baseball, basketball or one of the individual sports such as track and field or gymnastics? Back in the early 1970s, former two-time men's figure skating Olympic gold medalist Dick Button gave the proposition serious thought and developed a decathlon-type contest to determine the world's greatest athlete.

Button shopped the concept to the three major American television networks and eventually convinced ABC's Roone Arledge to televise the event. And so, in 1973, *Superstars* was born. This was an era before free agency. There were very few multiyear contracts, and only the elite athletes in the major team sports earned more than $100,000 a year, so the prize money at this event, held in Rotunda, would be a nice bonus for the participants who did well.

Originally broadcast as a two-hour special, the two-day event consisted of a 100-yard dash, an 800-meter run, weightlifting, bowling, tennis, rowing, basketball, a one-mile bicycle race, swimming and an obstacle course. In some years, certain events were dropped and replaced by baseball hitting and closest-to-the-pin golfing.

Olympic pole vaulter Bob Seagren won the first competition in 1973. One of the more memorable moments that year came when former heavyweight champion Joe Frazier nearly drowned during the swimming race. Not only had he never raced before, but Smokin' Joe later admitted that he also didn't know how to swim.

North American Soccer League star Kyle Rote Jr. was a three-time *Superstars* winner, and O.J. Simpson, one of many sports stars who competed while still in their prime, won the event in 1975.

Other notable competitors from pro football included Roger Staubach, Carl Eller, Lynn Swann, Jack Ham, Franco Harris and Johnny Unitas. Major League Baseball players included Lou Brock, Johnny Bench, Reggie Jackson, Mike Schmidt and Carl Yastrzemski. The NBA was represented by John Havlicek, Elvin Hayes, "Pistol" Pete Maravich and Bill Bradley. From hockey came Bobby Hull, Stan Makita, Rod Gilbert, Marcel Dionne, Bryan Trottier, Pete Mahovolich and Wayne Gretzky. Former Olympians included downhill skier Jean-Claude Killy, wrestler Dan Gable and track stars Jim Ryun, Renaldo Nehemiah, Dave Johnson, Rafer Johnson, Bill Toomey and Bob Beamon.

There were usually three separate preliminary competitions held a week apart, with the top three winners advancing to a final round. All of the athletes listed above were future Hall of Fame athletes, Olympic gold medalists or world record holders. It's worth noting that two participants, Bill Bradley (Senator, D-NJ) and Jim Ryun (Congressman, R-KA) were elected to Congress after they retired.

Other noteworthy participants included race car drivers Johnny Rutherford and Emerson Fittipaldi, tennis players Rod Laver, Arthur Ashe and Bjorn Borg, and boxers Larry Holmes, Ken Norton and Bob Foster.

Women's Superstars

As the success of *Superstars* spread, a women's division was started. Some of the great athletes of the era who participated were Olympic champions Micki King (diving), Anne Henning (speed skating), Wyomia Tyus (track), Shirley Babashoff (swimming) and Ann Meyers (basketball). Tennis stars Althea Gibson and Martina Navratilova also entered the event.

Movie and TV Stars Become Superstars of Sport

Not satisfied with showcasing world-class male and female athletes, in 1975 and 1976, ABC also held a *Superstars* competition in which celebrities competed among themselves, with the top three finishers advancing to the finals against the athletes. Academy Award–winning actor Robert Duvall signed up, as did fellow actors Kevin Dobson (*Kojak*, *Knots Landing*), Robert Conrad (*The Wild Wild West*, *Baa, Baa Black Sheep*) and Lou Ferrigno (*The Incredible Hulk*). Other celebrities such as designer Oleg Cassini, singer Kenny Rogers and authors Peter Benchley (*Jaws*) and George Plimpton (*Paper Lion*) also competed. Duvall won the celebrity preliminary competition and finished sixth in a 15-man field against the pro athletes.

Chapter Eight

Floridians Who Left Their Mark

The scourge of racism robbed millions of black people of the opportunity to fulfill their potential. It also robbed society as a whole from being enriched by the full extent of their talents. In sports, one such man was Jake Gaither, the legendary football coach of Florida A&M University (FAMU) from 1945 to 1969. When Gaither retired after 25 years of leading the Rattlers, he had a winning percentage of .844, the highest of any college coach in history. Yet, when fans of college football discuss the sport's greatest coaches, you never hear his name being mentioned along with Bear Bryant, Joe Paterno or Bobby Bowden.

Had it not been for the Jim Crow era in which Gaither lived, the Knoxville College of Tennessee graduate would definitely have achieved greater notoriety. With an extraordinary record of consistency and excellence throughout his quarter century at A&M, today Gaither's name would be in the Rolodex of every major Division I athletic director in the nation. A coach who demanded, and achieved, superior play on the field and high moral character off it would be in great demand.

Gaither, a devout Christian, took his role as a mentor and educator seriously. Swearing was forbidden, and in his dual role as a teacher and the school's athletic director, he insisted that his players graduate. Gaither also earned a master's degree in physical education and health from Ohio State. And his wife, Sadie, who taught English at A&M, helped him ride herd on the Rattler players. Today, Gaither would scoff at the notion that schools such as Notre Dame and Penn State can't maintain BCS-caliber teams because of their high academic standards.

Thirty-six players from Gaither's teams were All-Americans, and 42 went on to play in the NFL. During his 25 years as head coach, FAMU won 22 Southern Intercollegiate Athletic Conference championships. Gaither's teams also won six black college national championships, in 1950, 1952, 1954, 1957, 1959 and 1961. He liked to say that he recruited players who were "agile, mobile and hostile."

Some of his more noteworthy players who went on to greater glory include Pro Football Hall of Fame wide receiver and Olympic sprinter Bob Hayes of the Dallas Cowboys, Cincinnati defensive back Ken Riley, who ranks fifth on the NFL's all-time list in interceptions, and speedster Willie Galimore, an All-Pro running back with the Chicago Bears in the late 1950s and early 1960s. One of his non-football disciples was tennis great Althea Gibson, a 1953 graduate of A&M.

When Gaither retired from coaching in 1969 with a record of 204–36–4, he was just the fourth coach to reach the 200-win plateau. What's all the more remarkable is that the Rattlers never played more than 10 games a season; today's teams usually play 12 or 13.

Gaither outlived Jim Crow and was bestowed with countless honors and awards. He was inducted to several college and other sports-related Halls of Fame before he died in 1994 at age 90.

Hayes is Golden on the Track

Sports fans are forever arguing about which athlete is the best at his or her respective position, the best in a particular sport and even the best overall athlete in the world. Quite a few Florida-based sports bar debates ensued when both ESPN and *Sports Illustrated* listed Bob Hayes in fifth place when ranking the Sunshine State's greatest athletes of the 20th century.

Atop both sports media giants' lists were Deion Sanders, Emmitt Smith, Chris Evert and Steve Carlton. These athletes are all worthy of consideration, but one achievement is missing from their résumés. As great as they all were, their greatness was confined to a single sport. The man known as "Bullet" was a two-time Olympic champion and world-record holder in track, as well as a Hall of Fame wide receiver in pro football.

In the early 1960s, this Jacksonville native was regarded as the top sprinter in the world, and with good reason. Bob Hayes set or tied world sprint records measured in both yards and meters. He was the first person to break six seconds in the 60-yard dash with his indoor world record of 5.9 seconds. While in college in 1962, Hayes also set a world record for the 100-yard dash, running the distance in 9.2 seconds.

A year later, he broke that mark with a time of 9.1 seconds, a record that stood for 11 years. Also in 1963, Hayes set the world best for the 200 meters (20.5 seconds, though the time was never ratified) and tied the world record for the 220-yard dash with a time of 20.6 seconds. He was the AAU champion in the 100-yard dash three years running, from 1962 to 1964, and in 1964, he was also the NCAA champion at 200 meters.

At the 1964 Summer Olympics in Tokyo, Hayes ran a world-record-tying 10.0 seconds in the 100 meters to win the gold medal—and the unofficial title of "World's Fastest Human." His performance running the anchor leg of the 4x100-meter relay was breathtaking. Hayes took the baton with the U.S. team in fifth place and blazed past four other world-class sprinters to give the Americans a world-record time of 39.06 seconds and earn Bullet Bob his second gold medal.

The Bullet on Target in the NFL

Although Bob Hayes shone on the world stage in track, he always maintained that football was his first love. He played on a state championship team in high school and was a star receiver and halfback for Jake Gaither's great Florida A&M teams. His football talent was evident enough that in 1964, the Dallas Cowboys drafted Hayes a year early, at a time when the NFL allowed teams to make "future" draft picks.

After winning two gold medals at the Olympic Games in Japan, Hayes returned to A&M for his final football season. In his last season of college ball, he scored touchdowns and extra points as a receiver and running back, which was good enough to earn him an invitation to the since-discontinued College All-Star Game, where college all-stars played the previous year's NFL champion at the beginning of training camp. It's worth noting that sharing the huddle with Hayes for that game was another Dallas future draft pick and teammate, quarterback Roger Staubach.

Hayes made an immediate impact during his rookie season in 1965. He quickly became a favorite target of Cowboys quarterback Don Meredith and led all NFL receivers in touchdown receptions in both of his first two seasons. Although zone defenses existed in 1965, Hayes' world-class speed forced defensive coordinators to hasten its further development. He led the NFL in yards per catch in 1970 and 1971 with a staggering 26.1 and 24.0, respectively.

Hayes set Dallas team records that still stand. He caught the longest touchdown pass, 95 yards, in team history during a game against Washington in 1966. In that same game, he finished with nine receptions for another record 246 yards and two touchdowns. Bullet Bob was voted to three Pro Bowls, played in two NFL championship games and was a member of the Cowboys' first two Super Bowl teams, including their 1971 championship squad.

Hayes retired as the all-time team leader in yards, receptions and touchdowns, though all three markers have since been passed. He is one of only three players in NFL history with at least 200 receptions averaging more than 20 yards per catch. (Homer Jones and Paul Warfield are the others.) And Hayes joins Jim Thorpe as the only member of the Pro Football Hall of Fame who has won not one, but two Olympic gold medals.

Faster Than the Bullet

In the early 1960s, Bob Hayes was known as the World's Fastest Human, and track aficionados were still talking about Bullet Bob a decade later, but the context changed in the spring of 1975.

Five hours due west of Jacksonville, just off U.S. Highway 10, a teen sensation named Houston McTear from the little town of Milligan ran the 100-yard dash in a world-record-tying 9.0 seconds on May 9, 1975, at the state High School Class AA track meet in Winter Park. And the 18-year-old's long jump of 24 feet, six inches was the longest by a high school athlete in 1975.

If that wasn't enough to grab one's attention, McTear was a standout on the gridiron as well. As a running back for the Baker High Gators, McTear gained 1380 yards on 96 carries in 1974, which was enough to draw the attention of Division I coaches at Florida, Florida State, Notre Dame, Nebraska and Alabama.

Much to the dismay of the football coaches, McTear opted to concentrate on track, where he was already favored to win a spot on the 1976 U.S. Olympic team. McTear made the team, but a hamstring injury prevented him from running, so he relocated to California to train, setting his sights on the 1980 Games in Moscow.

Fast Life Prevents Fast Times

In 1977, McTear ran the fastest 100-meter time (10.13 seconds) in America and the fastest 60 yards (6.05 seconds) in the world. In 1978, he set a world mark in the 60 meters (6.54 seconds) that stood until 1986, but more injuries and a fondness for the fast life off the track, which included cocaine, prevented him from making the 1980 Olympic team. By 1984, his career at the world level was a memory, and he spent several years homeless and hooked on drugs.

McTear's fortunes changed in the late 1980s when he met Linda Haglund, a former three-time Olympic sprinter from Sweden who was a track coach at Santa Monica College. With Haglund's help, McTear got back into training and won the 60 meters at the Swedish Indoor Championships in 1990 with a time of 6.68 seconds. According to Haglund, McTear turned in a 10.45 in 1991 and went on to win several races in Europe, but there would be no Olympic glory. The two athletes eventually married, and as of 2008, McTear was alive and well, living in Europe.

Boycott Interrupts But Doesn't Derail Dreams of Gold

Born in Iowa City, Iowa, in 1962, Nancy Hogshead moved to Jacksonville with her family when she was a child. She began swimming at age seven, and by her freshman year in high school, she held the distinction of being the only American swimmer ranked number one in the world (in the 200-meter butterfly).

A state champion at Episcopal High School in Jacksonville, she was the first woman to be offered a swimming scholarship at Duke University. Hogshead finished both her high school and college career undefeated in dual meet competition. She also excelled at an international level in both the butterfly and freestyle events, and as a member of several relay teams. She qualified for the 1980 U.S. Olympic team, but President Carter decided that the country would not participate in the Games to protest the Soviet Union's invasion of Afghanistan.

Shortly afterward, Hogshead retired from swimming and continued her academic studies at Duke. She had a change of heart in 1983 as the nation geared up for the 1984 Summer Games in Los Angeles. She was part of the 4x100-meter relay team that set a world record that year and was named Comeback Swimmer of the Year by USA Swimming.

At the Los Angeles Games, Hogshead won an individual gold in the 100-meter freestyle in an event final in which she finished in dead heat with fellow American Carrie Steinseifer. Unable to determine a winner, officials awarded gold medals to both swimmers. Hogshead finished second to teammate Tracey Caulkins in the 200-meter individual medley and anchored the winning 4x100 freestyle and 4x100 medley relay teams. Her four medals were the most of any swimmer at the 23rd Olympiad.

Medal Platform Used as a Springboard

One of the more tired clichés says that sports builds character, and to a degree, it does. But it also reveals character. In a race for a fifth medal in Los Angeles, Nancy Hogshead experienced a life-altering event. She suffered a bronchial spasm and finished fourth. Medical tests revealed that she had exercise-induced asthma, a condition that had unknowingly hindered her cardiovascular training for years.

Hogshead retired from competitive swimming and became a spokesman for the American Lung Association. She traveled the country, making appearances and giving lectures on living with and managing the condition. She even wrote a book, *Asthma and Exercise*.

After the Olympics, Hogshead returned to Duke and completed her degree in political science and women's studies. She then earned a law degree from Georgetown University and today is a practicing lawyer in Jacksonville, as well as a law professor at a local college. Her husband, Scott Makar, has been the Florida solicitor general since 2007. In her post-Olympic career, Hogshead swam against the stream for a righteous cause, as an exponent of Title IX, the 1972 federal law that states:

> "No person in the United States shall, on the basis of sex, be excluded from participation in, be denied the benefits of, or be subjected to discrimination under any education program or activity receiving Federal financial assistance..."

As an advocate for this cause, Hogshead has testified before Congress many times, co-authored a book on the subject entitled *Title IX and Social Change*, was an expert witness in Title IX court cases and has appeared or been profiled on the issue by CBS, CNN and ESPN.

Many people who attain a certain level of celebrity use that achievement to improve their station in life, which is perfectly fine. Others, like Nancy Hogshead, have used their platform as an opportunity to substantially improve and enrich the lives of others.

Sweet Lou and Smooth Tony

Half a century ago, the baseball fields of West Tampa produced two major league players who went on to become Hall of Fame–caliber managers. Lou Piniella and Tony LaRussa were teammates in the PONY League, and both men eventually played major league ball and guided teams to World Series championships.

There is no comparison in their playing careers. LaRussa was a seldom-used utility infielder who had just 176 at bats in six seasons over 11 years. Piniella was an American League Rookie of the Year, All-Star, seven-time .300 hitter and a starter for four AL pennant winners and two World Series champions. He was regarded as a clutch hitter, finished with a .291 career average and batted .305 in 44 playoff and World Series games.

As a manager, Piniella's famed temper tantrums, albeit entertaining, at times detracted from his otherwise very successful résumé as a manager. "Sweet Lou" had a winning record with four of the five teams that he skippered: Yankees (.537), Reds (.525), Mariners (.542) and Cubs (.519), including a major league record single-season best 116–46 in 2001 with Seattle. Only during his three-year trial with the poorly resourced Tampa Bay Devil Rays (.412) did he fail to produce an overall winning record. Yet, there was a highlight even with the Rays. The 2004 club that won 70 games was the first team in franchise history to win *as many as* 70 games and not finish in last place.

Piniella retired, for good he says, near the end of the 2010 season. He ranks 14th in career wins as a manager, with 1835; his teams won six division titles and finished second five times; he was named American League Manager of the Year twice with Seattle, in 1995 and 2001; he won the National League version of the award with Chicago in 2008; and his Reds swept LaRussa's A's in the 1990 World Series.

After his playing days ended in 1973, LaRussa earned a law degree from Florida State and began his career as a minor league coach and manager. His managerial debut in the major leagues came with the Chicago White Sox in 1979. His 1981 team qualified for the playoffs in the strike-shortened season, and it was the first time the White Sox had played postseason ball since their pennant-winning team of 1959. Chicago won its first and only AL West crown in 1983 but fell to the eventual world-champion Baltimore Orioles.

After a few poor seasons, LaRussa was canned during a losing 1986 campaign, only to be signed by Oakland to manage the A's a few weeks later. With Oakland, he had three consecutive pennant winners in 1988,

1989 and 1990, and swept the crosstown rival Giants to win the 1989 World Series.

His post-pennant-winning era in Oakland wasn't so successful, and LaRussa left to join the St. Louis Cardinals after the 1995 season. Since joining the Cardinals, LaRussa has guided the Redbirds to 12 winning seasons in 15 years, including two NL pennants and their only World Series championship since 1987.

At the close of the 2010 season, LaRussa ranked third in career wins (2638) behind John McGraw (2763) and Connie Mack (3731), whom he'll join one day in Cooperstown.

The Rams Stumble Upon a Future NFL Great

There are many ways to describe the play and the competitive character of David "Deacon" Jones: tough, tenacious, hungry, quick, strong, Spartan. It was those attributes that fueled an internal fire and produced the greatest pass rusher in NFL history.

The man who was called "The Secretary of Defense" had a simple, straightforward approach to playing football. As a defensive end, he would constantly attack and keep opposing players on the defensive. He claimed that this strategy enabled him to withstand 14 years of battling pro football's best offensive linemen in the trenches. After three years in high school, another four in college and 14 years in the pros, he retired without a lasting bump or bruise on his body.

Jones was born in 1938 in Eatonville, just five miles from Orlando. He starred in football, basketball and baseball at the all-black Hungerford High School. He split his college time between Mississippi Vocational (now Mississippi Valley State) and South Carolina State. It was at South Carolina that Jones was spotted by two scouts of the Los Angeles Rams who were reviewing game film of one of the Bulldogs' opponents. They took note of the lineman who was faster than the runners that they were scouting.

Luckily for the Rams, black schools were historically poorly scouted in the late 1950s, so when Jones became eligible to be drafted, the Rams made him a "sleeper" pick and chose the future Hall of Famer—in the 14th round.

The Sleeper Wakes Up

By his own admission, Jones was a raw talent. But he learned quickly, and by 1964, he began the first of seven consecutive Pro Bowl seasons. At left end, Jones anchored a defensive line, along with fellow Hall of Famers Merlin Olsen, Lamar Lundy and Rosey Grier, that was known throughout the NFL as the "Fearsome Foursome."

His philosophy was to bring ferocity and inflict physical pain on linemen, running backs and quarterbacks on every play. Jones went all out on each play and considers the "situation substitutions" employed by today's coaches to keep linemen fresh as, well, less than manly.

Jones wanted to intimidate his opponents for the entire game. He was recognized as the best in the league in catching quarterbacks attempting to pass. He even coined a term, "sack," to describe what he did to opposing quarterbacks. Although the NFL didn't officially keep such stats, all the teams did and so did the media. The league eventually began to recognize the quarterback sack, but not until 1982.

Jones' "unofficial" career total of pillaged quarterbacks was 173.5, all of which took place in 14-game seasons. The total ranks third, behind leader Bruce Smith (200) and Reggie White (198), both of whom played their careers in the current 16-game schedules.

One of Jones' techniques, the "head slap" was so effective (and infuriating) that offensive linemen lobbied for its abolition.

After an injury caused him to miss several games in 1971, Jones was traded to San Diego in 1972, where he became a team captain and returned to Pro Bowl form. He retired following the 1974 season and was elected to the Pro Football Hall of Fame in 1980, his first year of eligibility.

As a side note, when the Giants Michael Strahan set the single-season sack record of 22.5 in 2001, the last sack was against his friend, quarterback Brett Favre of the Packers in a meaningless game in the season finale for both teams. Favre purposely fell to the ground, and Strahan simply touched him to get credit for the record-setting sack. Such antics would have made Jones ill. After all, when describing what motivated him to coin the now-famous term, Jones said, "It's like when a conquering army sacks a city. Or it's like putting quarterbacks in a sack and hitting them with a baseball bat." Taking a dive may have been a courtesy by Favre, but it wouldn't have spared him against Jones.

From the Little Series to the Big Series

John Wesley "Boog" Powell was one of the best baseball prospects to come out of Florida in the 1950s. Born in Lakeland in 1941, Powell moved with his family to Key West when he was a teenager. The future Baltimore Orioles star acquired his nickname from his father; many southerners called mischievous kids "little buggers," so his dad shortened it to Boog. Powell said that he'd been called Boog all his life and wouldn't know to respond if someone called him John.

Powell's exceptional baseball talent was evident even when he was a young boy. At age 12, Boog and his two brothers, Charlie and Carl, played on the Lakeland team that went to the 1954 Little League World Series in Williamsport, Pennsylvania. Lakeland lost 16–0 in the quarterfinals to the eventual champion team from Schenectady, New York.

A three-sport star for the local Key West Conch's high school teams, Powell earned letters in baseball, football and basketball. He was recruited by several colleges but decided instead to sign a minor league contract with the Baltimore Orioles and joined their farm system in 1959. After three years in the minors, Powell was brought up at the end of the 1961 season and, one year later, became Baltimore's starting first baseman in 1962 when he was just 20 years old.

Over the next 14 seasons, he was a mainstay in the Orioles lineup. A four-time American League All-Star, Powell played in four World Series, including the Orioles championship teams of 1966 and 1970. During the 1966 season, in which he finished third in the MVP voting, Powell had two "career" days.

In a double-header on July 6, 1966, he drove in a team-record seven runs in the opener and four more in the nightcap for 11 RBIs, which tied the American League record. Five weeks later, on August 16, he victimized the Red Sox by belting three home runs for a 4–2 win; it was the third time in his career that he had turned the feat. The other two occasions occurred against the Washington Senators on August 10, 1963 (a 6–5 loss), and on June 27, 1964 (a 3–1 win).

His best season came in 1970 when he hit 35 home runs, drove in 114 runs, batted .297 and was named the American League's Most Valuable Player. Powell was traded to Cleveland in 1975 and spent two seasons with the Indians before retiring in 1977 as a member of the Dodgers. He finished his career with 339 home runs, 1187 RBIs and a .266 batting average.

Today, Powell is the owner of the popular eatery Boog's BBQ, an outdoor barbecue stand located behind the centerfield bleachers on Eutaw Street at Camden Yards in Baltimore, Maryland. It has been a must-see for baseball fans and tourists since the stadium opened in 1992.

That Was Some Storm

Most tropical storms that wreak havoc in the U.S. usually hit South Florida first. Those that don't dissipate continue on to cause damage in other parts of the country. In a strictly sporting sense, Steve "Lefty" Carlton's baseball career followed a similar path and inflicted severe damage to the psyche of the major league hitters he faced.

After a successful career as a pitcher at North Miami High School and Miami-Dade College, Carlton was signed by the St. Louis Cardinals in 1963 at age 19. Signed for the bargain price of $5000, he went to the Cards' minor league team in Rock Hill, North Carolina, where he was 10–1. After two more stops on the junior circuit, he was pitching in the big leagues.

Carlton's major league debut was uneventful for perhaps everyone but him. On opening day of the 1965 season against the Cubs, he walked the only batter he faced in the 11th inning of a game at Wrigley Field.

He pitched sparingly for the rest of season and was sent back to the minors. He was recalled for good midway through the 1966 season and became a significant member of the Cardinals World Series championship team of 1967, going 14–9 with a 2.98 ERA. He made the National League All-Star team in 1968 when St. Louis won the pennant, but the team fell to the Detroit Tigers in seven games in the World Series.

But it was during the 1969 season that the baseball world really took notice. Against the Mets on September 15, Carlton struck out a then–major league record 19 batters in a 4–3 loss to the Mets. On a night when Lefty appeared untouchable, New York outfielder Ron Swaboda hit not one, but two, two-run homers.

Carlton had a disastrous 1970 season but bounced back to go 20–9 in 1971. A bitter contract dispute with St. Louis management prompted the Cardinals to trade him to the last-place team in the National League East Division, the Philadelphia Phillies.

Sweet Revenge

Frustrated in contract negotiations with Carlton, the Cardinals' management dealt its new ace to the Phillies for Rick Wise, who was also in a contract standoff with Phillies' management. As far as the players were concerned, it appeared that Wise got the better of the deal. He was going from one of the worst teams in baseball to a contender.

For Carlton, who was coming off his best season, it would be a struggle to repeat as a 20-game winner. And it was. Despite pitching for a team that was 19th out of 24 in runs scored, Philadelphia's new star went 27–10 with a 1.97 ERA and became the first pitcher to win a Cy Young Award for a last-place team. Carlton accounted for a record 45.8 percent of Philadelphia's 59 wins in 1972, while Wise went 16–16 with a 3.11 ERA for a mediocre St. Louis team that finished in fourth place.

Carlton struggled in 1973 but then strung together nine consecutive winning seasons, which included four more 20-game winning campaigns, as well as pocketing the rest of his NL-record four Cy Young Awards.

After back-to-back losing seasons, the Phillies released Carlton during the 1986 season. He played for the San Francisco Giants, Chicago White Sox, Cleveland Indians and Minnesota Twins before retiring in 1988. When he finally left the game, the 10-time All-Star's ledger for 24 seasons read 329 wins, 244 losses and a 3.22 ERA. He pitched in four World Series and for two World Series champions. Carlton had 4136 strikeouts, which ranks fourth behind Nolan Ryan, Randy Johnson and Roger Clemens, respectively. Lefty was elected to the Hall of Fame in 1994, his first year of eligibility.

Save Me a Place...I'll Be Back

After throwing just 25 innings for the Cardinals in 1965, Carlton was sent down to the minors to the parent club's Tulsa, Oklahoma, affiliate for the 1966 season. In July, the 20-year-old was tabbed to start the annual Hall of Fame exhibition game in Cooperstown as part of the induction weekend's festivities.

Facing the defending American League champion Minnesota Twins, Carlton went the distance and picked up the win. More importantly, he was recalled to the big leagues for good.

Carlton Outdueled by Tom Terrific

From 1970 to 1983, Lefty had a great professional rivalry with the best right-handed starter in the game, Tom Seaver, who pitched for the New York Mets and the Cincinnati Reds. By 1970, Seaver had replaced Bob Gibson as the premier right-handed starter in baseball. The Hall of Fame hurler became a five-time 20-game winner, won three Cy Young Awards and finished his career with 311 wins and 3640 strikeouts.

Over 14 seasons, the two power-throwing aces squared off 17 times, with Seaver enjoying a prohibitive edge, 11–3. During this span, Carlton enjoyed all six of his 20-game winning seasons and was one of the most successful starters in the game (253–166). His record in these duels was 3–13.

Five Doors Close, One Opens

Many of the world's greatest athletes were born with superior athletic talent that was evident from an early age and continued uninterrupted on their way to individual or team championships at the amateur, collegiate and professional levels. For others, like Rowdy Gaines, the path was less certain. Born in Winter Haven in 1959, Haines was interested in sports in high school and tried out for the football team, but when he didn't make the cut, he turned to the basketball team. No luck. He received the same response when he tried to make the baseball team.

Having exhausted his options in team sports, he turned to individual outlets such as golf and tennis, which are less subjective when evaluating raw talent. But Gaines was told he didn't have what it took in either of those two activities. With his options shrinking, there were just track and swimming left, and Gaines opted for the water.

He barely qualified for one of Winter Haven High School's relay teams, but he raised a few eyebrows in his first meet when he swam the fastest split on the team. A career was born, but Gaines had some catching up to do since most of the world's great swimmers start the sport as children. The clock doesn't lie for swimmers or runners. Knowing that he had earned a spot on the swim team, Gaines dedicated himself to maximizing his potential and earned a scholarship to Auburn University.

In college, he was a five-time NCAA champion and a 22-time All-American. By the spring of 1980, Gaines was acknowledged as the fastest swimmer in the world and was a favorite to win five gold medals at the Olympics that summer in Moscow. But it was not to be—the U.S. decided not to send a team to the games in protest of the USSR's invasion of Afghanistan in 1979.

With his dreams of Olympic glory crushed and his college career ending a year later, Gaines temporarily stopped swimming. But he soon returned to the water and focused on winning gold at the 1984 Games in Los Angeles. It was not a sure thing. Although Gaines made the team, the times he swam at the Olympic Trials were not impressive, and he was not expected to be a factor in Los Angeles.

At the 1984 Olympics, Gaines won three gold medals, one in the 100-meter freestyle and the other two on record-setting relay teams in the 4x100 freestyle and the 4x100 medley. The kid who was repeatedly cut by a string of high school coaches seized the moment and made it his.

Still Battling, and Beating, Adversaries

After the Olympics, Gaines stayed in swimming and began competing on the "senior" or masters circuit. Shortly after a masters event in 1991, Gaines got the scare of his life when he became temporarily paralyzed with Guillain-Barré syndrome, a rare autoimmune disorder that affects the peripheral nervous system. He spent several months in the hospital and underwent extensive rehabilitation to regain the use of his arms and legs. Gaines eventually achieved full recovery and returned to the pool. In 1996, at age 35, he qualified for the Olympic Trials for that year's Summer Games in Atlanta but decided not to compete.

Gaines' involvement with swimming continues to this day as a television commentator, fundraiser, youth charity supporter and, of course, as a competitor.

In October 2010, the 51-year-old Gaines swam on the world record-setting 200-meter freestyle relay team at a masters-level meet in Orlando. It was his 40th world record in a masters event.

Barber Drops His Mop for a Mike

Although Walter Lanier "Red" Barber never played professional or college sports, he painted a picture for the many fans who "watched" sporting events on their radios from the 1930s through the 1960s. Barber was born in 1908, in Columbus, Mississippi, but moved to Sanford as a boy. At 18, he hitchhiked to Gainesville to enroll at the University of Florida to study education.

At UF, he held a part-time job as a janitor. When a professor failed to appear to read a scholarly paper over the air on the campus radio station, WRUF, Barber jumped in to fill the void. He was a natural on the air, and his mop and broom were forever replaced by a microphone. He was soon broadcasting Gator football games and eventually became director for the station.

Barber soon dropped out of school to pursue his new vocation full time. A few years later, he was hired to be the play-by-play announcer for the Cincinnati Reds.

After five years in Cincinnati, Barber joined the Brooklyn Dodgers, and it was calling Dodgers games that gained him national stature. In the 1940s, he became the sports director for the CBS Radio Network. While at CBS, Barber hired a young Fordham University graduate, Vin Scully, who eventually joined the Dodgers' broadcast team.

In 1954, Barber left the Dodgers and jumped to the hated crosstown rival Yankees, where he was teamed with Mel Allen, himself a broadcasting icon, and former Yankee shortstop Phil Rizzuto. Barber's contract with the Yanks was not renewed following the 1966 season. He went into semi-retirement, writing several books, and from 1981 until his death in 1992, he was a regular contributor to National Public Radio's *Morning Edition* program.

Barber was honored by the university that launched his career, even though he never graduated. In 1979, he received a Distinguished Alumni Award, and the university's College of Journalism and Broadcasting awards the Red Barber Radio Scholarship each year to a student studying sports broadcasting.

Among Barber's many honors is the Ford C. Frick Award from the Baseball Hall of Fame. Barber and Allen were the first recipients of the award, which is presented annually by the Hall of Fame to a broadcaster for "major contributions to baseball." The Hall further honored Barber by displaying the microphone that he used at WRUF in its "Scribes and Mikemen" exhibit. Shortly before his death, Barber donated his vast collection of writings, scrapbooks, correspondence and manuscripts from the 1920s to the 1990s to his alma mater.

Summerall Shines in All Seasons

Pat Summerall attained similar stature to Barber behind a microphone, but unlike Red, the man who teamed with John Madden for more than two decades was also a participant in several sports. George Allen "Pat" Summerall was born in Lake City in 1930 and excelled in football, baseball, basketball and tennis at Columbia High School. He earned three letters in football and basketball and two in baseball. He also won the Florida State Tennis championship and twice achieved All-State basketball honors.

Summerall went on to be a two-sport star in football and basketball at the University of Arkansas. He was a two-way star defensive end, tight end and placekicker, and was a two-time All Southwest Conference selection in both sports.

Drafted by the Detroit Lions in the fourth round of the 1952 NFL draft, he played 10 seasons as a kicker for the Lions, Chicago Cardinals and New York Giants. The highlight of Summerall's NFL career came in the final week of the 1958 season. His 49-yard field goal as time expired gave the Giants a 13–10 win over Cleveland and sent New York to the playoffs. Two weeks later, Summerall kicked a field goal and two extra points in New York's epic 23–17 overtime loss to Baltimore in the NFL championship game.

Summerall moved to the broadcasting booth upon his retirement following the 1961 season and began a career as a radio announcer and expert commentator for football television broadcasts at CBS. It was clear that the college-educated Summerall, who also held a master's degree in Russian history, was capable of breaking the mold of the "ex-jock" in the booth as he became the network's chief play-by-play announcer for football, tennis and golf.

In the mid-1970s, Summerall was paired with former Philadelphia Eagles defensive back Tom Brookshire, and the two became the most popular television sports team over the next few years.

In 1981, CBS broke up the Summerall–Brookshire tandem and teamed Pat with former Oakland Raiders coach John Madden. The popularity he had earned with Brookshire was surpassed with his new partner. Summerall, who was known for his straightforward, economy-of-words style, was complimented by Madden's more lively and emotional personality. The partnership, which lasted 22 years, stayed intact when Summerall and Madden jumped to the Fox Network when CBS lost broadcast rights after the 1993 season. Summerall also provided commentary for the first few years of the popular video game *Madden NFL*, which is produced annually by EA Sports.

Not a White Guy, But the Right Guy

Bill White was a successful sports broadcaster who shared several qualities of both Barber and Summerall. He had an easy, down-home delivery similar to Barber, and like Summerall, his days as an eight-time, Major League All-Star first baseman lent authority to any opinion he might share.

The one major difference in the three is that Barber and Summerall were white, whereas White was black. Born William De Kova White to sharecroppers in Lakewood in 1934, he and his family eventually moved north to Warren, Ohio, where Bill was a standout athlete. He was signed by the New York Giants in 1952 and was shocked when he reported to the team's minor league club in North Carolina.

White was only the second African American player to be recruited for the team, and the locals didn't care what team he played for—all that mattered was his skin color. White recalled those days as some of the worst of his life.

The insulting racial epithets he heard, which would make his blood boil, didn't bother him as much as having to endure such injustices as waiting on the team bus while the white players went into a restaurant and ate, not being allowed to use the restroom at gas stations and not being permitted to stay in a decent hotel. Those painful memories remained undimmed by the passage of time.

Years later, as an All-Star first baseman, he began speaking out about the same types of injustices that black major leaguers were subjected to during spring training in Florida. Eventually, buttressed by pressure from the Cardinals organization, things began to change.

In a 13-year career with the Giants, Cardinals and Phillies, White was an eight-time National League All-Star and a seven-time Gold Glove winner for excellence in fielding, and four times he batted over .300 and drove in 100 runs. He is also a member of an exclusive club of just 107 players in Major League Baseball history who hit a home run in their first at bat in the big leagues.

During his career in St. Louis and Philadelphia, White entered the world of radio, hosting his own sports talk show. Just two years after his retirement, White joined the Yankees broadcasting team, and he announced games on radio and television from 1971 to 1988. He was the first African American to be a regular commentator for a professional sports team.

While with the Yankees, White was regarded as one of the top voices in the game. He was frequently tapped for postseason assignments when his Yankees contract allowed it. Having built a stellar reputation during his four decades in baseball, White was offered the position of president of the National League in 1989 and became the highest-ranking African American sports official in America. He remained in the post until he retired in 1994.

Waiting and Wondering

The voting process for each sports Hall of Fame differs. Each method has its strengths and shortcomings, and every year, when a particular sport announces its next class of inductees, there are bound to be stories about a deserving athlete or athletes who were passed over.

Chipley native Artis "The A-Train" Gilmore knows this quite well. For some reason, this 11-time All-Star in the ABA and NBA is not in the James A. Naismith Hall of Fame, better known as the Basketball Hall of Fame.

The hoop hall is different from others in that it enshrines not just American professional players, but players, coaches and significant contributors from around the world at virtually every level. So Gilmore and many of his teammates, coaches and opponents are baffled by the omission of a player who dominated the game at both the collegiate and pro levels.

Gilmore, who was a forbidding seven feet, two inches and 255 pounds on the floor, averaged more than 20 points and 20 rebounds per game at tiny Jacksonville University; he is one of only five players in NCAA history in the 20–20 club. In 1970, the Dolphins went 27–2 and averaged more than 100 points per game en route to a showdown with John Wooden's UCLA Bruins in the NCAA championship game. At the time, UCLA was in the middle of a record run of nine consecutive national championships. JU fell to the Bruins 80–69, but it was a remarkable accomplishment for a university that few outside Jacksonville had ever heard of.

After leaving JU, the A-Train joined the Kentucky Colonels of the ABA, where he won Rookie of the Year and MVP honors in the 1971–72 season. He was an ABA All-Star all five years that he played in the league and was the MVP of the 1975 ABA playoffs when he averaged 24 points and 17 rebounds per game. That year, he also led Kentucky to a 58–26 record as the Colonels defeated the Indiana Pacers in five games to win the league championship. Gilmore is generally considered the second-best player in league history, next to Julius Irving.

When the ABA folded, Gilmore joined the NBA and played for the Chicago Bulls, San Antonio Spurs and Boston Celtics. He was a four-time NBA All-Star with Chicago and twice with San Antonio. When he left the game, his combined ABA/NBA totals placed him as the 20th all-time scorer and fifth in career rebounds in pro basketball history. Many former players who are Hall of Famers themselves, such as Bill Walton, Dan Issel, George Gervin, Dominique Wilkins and coaches Hubie Brown and George Karl, have voiced their opinion in favor of Gilmore's induction.

All 19 of the players who scored more points than the A-Train and are eligible for the Hall of Fame have been inducted; the same goes for the 15 behind him. And only Wilt Chamberlain, Bill Russell, Moses Malone and Kareem Abdul-Jabbar have grabbed more rebounds.

Today, Gilmore works at his alma mater as an assistant to the president and waits for the right thing to be done. Unfortunately, it remains one of the sport's biggest mysteries as to why, nearly three decades after his retirement, this acknowledged great player, with no controversial episodes blemishing his career, is still waiting for his call to the Hall.

An Inspirational Life

Brian Piccolo, a running back for the Chicago Bears in the late 1960s, died of cancer at the age of 26. He never rushed for 1000 yards in a season during his brief career, nor was he given consideration when sportswriters voted for postseason awards and All-Pro teams. Instead, the Fort Lauderdale native's enduring legacy is one of uncommon decency, integrity and courage. In 1971, the story of his friendship with teammate Gale Sayers was made into an Emmy Award–winning television movie called *Brian's Song*.

Piccolo was a star runner at Central Catholic High School in Fort Lauderdale and earned a scholarship to play football at Wake Forest in North Carolina. In his senior season, he led the nation in rushing and scoring and was the Atlantic Coast Conference Player of the Year for 1964. But he went undrafted because pro teams thought the 5-foot-11, 190-pounder lacked the size and speed to make it in the NFL.

Piccolo signed a free agent contract with the Bears, who had drafted two-time All-American Sayers in the first round. Piccolo pulled a hamstring trying to make the team his rookie year and spent the 1965 season on the practice squad, which was called the "taxi squad" at the time. Meanwhile, Sayers was named NFL Rookie of the Year.

Although Piccolo made the team in 1966 as a backup to Sayers, he played mostly on special teams. In 1967, it was decided that the two would room together when the team traveled for away games. This was noteworthy at the time because Piccolo was white and Sayers was black—they were the first mixed-race roommates in the league. What seems absurdly trivial today was a very big deal at the time.

At that time, the Civil Rights movement was at its zenith. Martin Luther King Jr. made his famous "I Have a Dream" speech just four years earlier in 1963, and a year later, President Johnson signed the Civil Rights Act into law.

The anxiety of team and league officials was misplaced, as Piccolo and Sayers became best friends. Piccolo's playing time increased in 1967, and he became a starter midway though the 1968 season when Sayers was sidelined for the rest of the campaign with a knee injury.

During the 1969 season, Piccolo began to feel unwell. He had a persistent cough that continued to get worse, and he eventually removed himself from a game on November 16 against Atlanta. He went to see a doctor, and X-rays revealed that he had a tumor on his lung. He underwent surgery on November 28 and in April 1970.

A few weeks later, in May, Sayers was honored at a banquet in New York as the recipient of the George Halas Award as the league's most courageous player, credited for leading the NFL in rushing in 1969, when he returned from his 1968 injury-shortened season. When Sayers went to the podium, he gave a moving speech, stating that his friend and teammate, Brian Piccolo, was more deserving of the award. He ended the speech with the words, "I love Brian Piccolo, and I'd like all of you to love him, too. Tonight, when you hit your knees, please ask God to love him."

Despite the best efforts of the medical community, the cancer spread to other organs, and Brian Piccolo died on June 16, 1970. Thanks in part to the millions of dollars raised in Piccolo's name by family members and friends for cancer research, the disease that took his life has a high survival rate today.

Brian Piccolo and Darren Hill

The story of Brian Piccolo's brief career and his friendship was told beautifully in the movie *Brain's Song*, but an incident that took place during his college career at Wake Forest University is even more revealing of the man's character and decency.

Darryl Hill was a wide receiver for the University of Maryland in 1963. He was the first black player for the Terrapins and the first black player in the Atlantic Coast Conference.

Hill received support from his coaches and teammates but was the target of ugly racial slurs at road games and even received death threats in the mail. Hill and his teammates were physically attacked by racist fans at the stadium when they played South Carolina in Columbia. The atmosphere wasn't much better when Maryland played Wake Forest later in the year in Winston-Salem, North Carolina.

The crowd was giving it to Hill during the pregame warm-up, and as the warm-up ended, Hill noticed the Wake Forest team captain walking toward him.

"I want to apologize for the behavior of my fans," the other player said to Hill. He then placed his arm around Hill's shoulder, and escorted him toward the

Wake Forest side of the field where the taunting was at its worst. By the time they reached the middle of the field, the crowd had stopped its ugly behavior.

The Wake Forest captain was Brian Piccolo.

Chapter Nine

Florida Sports Hall of Fame Members

The Florida Sports Hall of Fame is located in Auburndale, halfway between Tampa and Orlando.

A list of abbreviations for universities and leagues appears at the end of this section.

Football

Anderson, Ottis (UM, NFL)
Biletnikoff, Fred (FSU, NFL, PFHOF)
Boselli, Tony (NFL)
Bowden, Bobby (FSU coach, CFHOF)
Brantley, Scot (UF, NFL)
Brooks, Derrick (FSU, NFL)
Buoniconti, Nick (NFL, PFHOF)
Casares, Rick (UF, NFL)
Collinsworth, Cris (UF, NFL)
Corso, Lee (FSU, college coach, broadcaster)
Csonka, Larry (NFL, PFHOF)
Curci, Fran (UM, college coach)
Casey, Charles (UF)
Chandler, Wes (UF, NFL)

Cox, Gene (FSU, high school coach)
Culverhouse, Hugh (NFL Tampa Bay owner)
Dooley, Jim (UM, college coach)
Everett, James (FAMU)
Farrior, J. Rex (UF, high school coach)
Ferguson, Forrest "Fergie" (UF)
Fleming, Don (UF, NFL)
Galimore, Willie (FAMU, NFL, CFHOF)
Gaither, Jake (FAMU coach, CFHOF)
Graves, Ray (UF coach, CFHOF)
Griese, Bob (NFL, CFHOF, PFHOF)
Gustafson, Andy (UM coach, CFHOF)
Harding, Jack (UM coach, CFHOF)
Higgins, Nash (U of Tampa coach)
Huerta, Marcelino (UF, college coach)
Hendricks, Ted (UM, NFL CFHOF, PFHOF)
Huizenga, H. Wayne (NFL Miami owner)
Johnson, Jimmy (UM, NFL coach)
Jones, Deacon (Florida native, NFL, PFHOF)
Irvin, Michael (UM, NFL, PFHOF)
Kelly, Jim (UM QB, NFL, PFHOF)
Kotys, Nick (South Florida high school coach)
Kosar, Bernie (UM, NFL)
Little, Larry (Bethune-Cookman, NFL, PFHOF)
Marino, Dan (NFL, CFHOF, PFHOF)
Masterson, Bob (UM, NFL)
McDowell, Jack (CFBHOF)
Moss, Perry (UM coach, FSU coach)
Mayberry, Walter (UF)
Mira, George (UM, NFL)
Moore, Nat (UF, NFL)

Nugent, Tom (FSU coach)
Pace, Dick (college football referee, administrator)
Peterson, Bill (FSU coach)
Quinn, Paul (high school coach)
Riley, Ken (FAMU, NFL)
Robbie, Joe (NFL Miami owner)
Selmon, Lee Roy (NFL, CFHOF, PFHOF)
Solomon, Freddie (U of Tampa, NFL)
Sellers, Ron (FSU, NFL, CFHOF)
Shula, Don (NFL, PFHOF)
Smith, Emmitt (UF, NFL, PFHOF, CFHOF)
Spurrier, Steve (UF, CFHOF)
Tate, Charlie (UM coach)
Testaverde, Vinny (UM, NFL)
Torretta, Gino (UM, NFL, CFHOF)
Van Fleet, General James (UF coach)
Veller, Don (FSU coach)
Van Sickel, Dale (UF coach)
Warfield, Paul (NFL, PFHOF)
Yepremian, Garo (NFL)
Youngblood, Jack (UF, NFL, CFHOF, PFHOF)

CFHOF: *College Football Hall of Fame, South Bend, Indiana*
PFHOF: *Pro Football Hall of Fame, Canton, Ohio*

Auto Racing

Allison, Bobby (NASCAR, NASCARHOF)
France Sr., Bill (NASCAR founder, NASCARHOF)
Frankman, Betty Skelton (land-speed racer)
Gregg, Peter (sports car racer)
Garlits, Don "Big Daddy" (Florida native, drag racer, IDRHOF)

Haywood, Hurley (sports car racer)
Roberts, Glenn "Fireball" (Florida native, NASCAR driver)
Rathmann, Jim (Indy 500 driver, ARHOF)
St. James, Lyn (race car driver)

ARHOF: *Auto Racing Hall of Fame, Indianapolis, Indiana*
IDRHOF: *International Drag Racing Hall of Fame, Ocala, Florida*
NASCARHOF: *NASCAR Hall of Fame, Charlotte, North Carolina*

Baseball

Boggs, Wade (Florida native, MLB, NBHOF)
Burdette, Lew (MLB)
Carlton, Steve (Florida native, MLB, NBHOF)
Carter, Gary (MLB, NBHOF)
Coleman, Vince (MLB)
Dawson, Andre (Florida native, MLB, NBHOF)
Fraser, Ron (UM coach)
Garvey, Steve (Florida native, MLB)
Geraghty, Ben (minor league manager)
Hutchinson, Fred (MLB pitcher, manager)
Howser, Dick (FSU, MLB player and manager)
Johnson, Davey (MLB player and manager)
Lang, Al (pioneered MLB spring training in Florida)
Lloyd, John "Pop" (Negro Leagues, NBHOF)
Lopez, Al (Florida native, MLB, NBHOF)
McGriff, Fred (MLB)
McRae, Hal (FAMU, MLB)
Martinez, Tino (Florida native, MLB)

Piniella, Lou (Florida native, MLB player and manager)
Powell, John "Boog" (Florida native, MLB)
Raines, Tim (Florida native, MLB)
Roberts, Robin (MLB, NBHOF)
Rosen, Al (UF, MLB player and administrator, NBHOF)
Score, Herb (Florida native, MLB player and broadcaster)
Smeltzy, Hal (Florida Southern coach)
Steinbrenner, George (MLB NY Yankees owner)
Sutton, Don (Florida native, MLB, NBHOF)
Sewell, "Rip" (Florida native, MLB "Eephus" pitcher)
Williams, Ted (MLB, NBHOF)
Waner, Paul (MLB, NBHOF)
Wynn, Early (MLB, NBHOF)

NBHOF: National Baseball Hall of Fame, Cooperstown, New York

Basketball

Barry, Rick (UM, NBA, NMBHOF)
Birdsong, Otis (Florida native, NBA)
Clark, Torchy (UCF coach)
Cowens, Dave (FSU, NBA, NMBHOF)
Dawkins, Darryl (Florida native, NBA)
Durham, Hugh (FSU grad and coach)
Fields, Joe (community college coach)
Gilmore, Artis (JU, ABA/NBA)
Strickland, Roger (JU, NBA)
Vitale, Dick (NCAA, NBA coach, broadcaster)
Wallen, Don (high school coach)
Wilkes, Glenn (Stetson University coach)

NMBHOF: Naismith Memorial Basketball Hall of Fame, Springfield, Massachusetts

Bowling

Carter, Don (IBMHOF)

IBHOF: *International Bowling Museum and Hall of Fame, Arlington, Texas*

Boxing

Dundee, Angelo (trainer, IBHOF)
Flynn, Ed (Florida native, Olympics)
Jackson, Julian E. (world champion boxer)

IBHOF: *International Boxing Hall of Fame, Canastota, New York*

Golf

Beman, Deane (PGA Tour commissioner, WGHOF)
Boros, Julius (PGA, WGHOF)
Bradley, Pat (LPGA Tour, WGHOF)
Berg, Patty (LPGA Tour, WGHOF)
Bolt, Tommy (PGA, WGHOF)
Carner, Joanne (LPGA Tour, WGHOF)
Cooper, Pete (PGA)
Floyd, Raymond (PGA, WGHOF)
Mayer, Dick (PGA)
Murphy, Bob (UF, PGA Tour)
Nicklaus, Jack (PGA Tour, WGHOF)
Norman, Greg (PGA Tour, WGHOF)
Owens, Charlie (PGA Tour)
Palmer, Arnold (PGA Tour, WGHOF)
Rodriquez, Chi Chi (PGA Tour, WGHOF)
Sanders, Doug (UF, PGA Tour)

Sarazen, Gene (PGA Tour, WGHOF)
Zaharias, Babe (LPGA Tour, WGHOF)

WGHOF: World Golf Hall of Fame, St. Augustine, Florida

Hockey

Andreychuk, Dave (NHL Tampa Bay)

Horse Racing

Hartack, Bill (jockey, NMRHOF)
Needles (Kentucky Derby winner, NRHOF)

National Museum of Racing Hall of Fame, Saratoga Springs, New York

Media

Barber, Walter "Red" (UF, broadcaster)
Boggs, Otis (UF, broadcaster)
Buchalter, Bill (sportswriter)
Gowdy, Curt (broadcaster)
McEwen, Tom (sportswriter)
Mizell, Hubert (sportswriter)
McGrotha, Bill (sportswriter)
Olsen, George (sports photographer)
Pope, Edwin (sportswriter)
Summerall, Pat (Florida native, broadcaster)
Taylor, Zack (sportswriter)

Promoters and Executives

Golden, Lafayette (FSHAA)
Lay, Floyd E. (FSHAA director, 1962–1980)
Pace, Dick (football referee, administrator)
Rosen, Al (UF, MLB administrator)
Seiler, Earnie (City of Miami recreation director, Orange Bowl)
Collins, Jerry (greyhound track owner)

Soccer

Akers, Michelle (UCF, Women's World Cup, Olympics, NSHOF)

NSHOF: National Soccer Hall of Fame and Museum, Oneonta, New York

Softball

Dudley, Herb (Florida native, Men's Fast Pitch, NSHOF)
Richardson, Dot (Florida native, Women's Fast Pitch, NSHOF)

NSHOF: National Softball Hall of Fame, Oklahoma City, Oklahoma

Swimming

Caulkins, Tracey (UF, Olympics, ISHOF)
Gaines, Rowdy (Florida native, Olympics, ISHOF)
Hogshead, Nancy (Florida native, Olympics, ISHOF)
Nelson, Jack (Olympics, Olympic coach, ISHOF)

Perry, Newton (UF swimmer and diver, swimming/ underwater acrobatics)

ISHOF: International Swimming Hall of Fame, Fort Lauderdale, Florida

Tennis

Courier, Jim (GSTC, ITHOF)
Evert, Chris (GSTC, ITHOF)
Fry, Shirley (GSTC, ITHOF)
Gibson, Althea (FAMU, GSTC, ITHOF)
Hart, Doris (UM, GSTC, ITHOF)
Mulloy, Gardnar (UM, GSTC, ITHOF)
Riggs, Bobby (GSTC, ITHOF)
Seles, Monica (GSTC, ITHOF)

GSTC: Grand Slam tournament Champion
ITHOF: International Tennis Hall of Fame, Newport, Rhode Island

Track and Field

Cheeseborough, Chandra (Florida native, Olympic sprinter, NTHOF)
Carnes, Jimmy (UF coach, Florida Track Club founder, NTHOF)
Hayes, Bob (FAMU, Olympic sprinter, PFHOF, NTHOF)
Pennel, John (Florida native, Olympic pole vaulter, NTHOF)
Shorter, Frank (UF, Olympic marathoner, NTHOF)

NTHOF: National Track & Field Hall of Fame, Indianapolis, Indiana

Volleyball

Wise, Mary (UF coach)

Water Sports

Aronow, Don (powerboat racer and builder)
Chenoweth, Dean (powerboat racer, MHOF)
Little, Bernie (powerboat racer)
Pope Jr., Dick (water skier, WSHOF)
Pope Sr., Dick (water skier, WSHOF)
Slater, Kelly (Florida native, surfer, SHOF)

MHOF: Motorsports Hall of Fame of America, Novi, Michigan
SHOF: Surfers Hall of Fame, Huntington Beach, California
WSHOF: Water Ski Hall of Fame, Polk City, Florida

Wrestling

Hogan, Hulk (Florida native, Wrestler, PWHOF)

PWHOF: Pro Wrestling Hall of Fame, Amsterdam, New York

Abbreviations for Universities and Leagues

ABA: American Basketball Association
FAMU: Florida A&M University
FSU: Florida State University
JU: Jacksonville University
LPGA: Ladies Pro Golf Association
MLB: Major League Baseball
NBA: National Basketball Association

NFL: National Football League
NHL: National Hockey League
PGA: Pro Golfers Association
UCF: University of Central Florida
UF: University of Florida
UM: University of Miami

Notes on Sources

Books

Bowden, Bobby and Mark Schlabach. *Called to Coach: Reflections on Life, Faith, and Football*. New York: Simon & Schuster, 2010.

Carroll, Bob, Michael Gershman, David Neft and John Thorn. *Total Football II: The Official Encyclopedia of the National Football League*. New York: HarperCollins, 1999.

Dooley, Pat. *Yesterday and Today: University of Florida Football*. Lincolnwood, IL: Publications International, 2009.

Dundee, Angelo. *My View from the Corner: A Life in Boxing*. New York: McGraw-Hill, 2008.

Feldman, Bruce. *Miami Football Vault: The History of the Miami Hurricanes*. Atlanta: Whitman Publishing, 2009.

Hinds, John. *Florida State Football Vault: The History of the Florida State Seminoles*. Atlanta: Whitman Publishing, 2008.

O'Toole, Andrew. *Paul Brown: The Rise and Fall and Rise Again of Football's Most Innovative Coach*. Cincinnati: Clerisy Press, 2008.

Pacheco, Ferdie. *Muhammad Ali: My View from the Corner*. New York: Birch Lane Press, 1992.

Porter, David L. *African-American Sports Greats: A Biographical Dictionary*. Westport, CT: Greenwood Publishing Group, 1995.

Thompson, Neal. *Driving with the Devil: Southern Moonshine, Detroit Wheels, and the Birth of NASCAR*. New York: Crown Publishing Group, 2007.

Print Sources

Baseball Digest
ESPN, The Magazine
Los Angeles Times
Miami Herald
New York Times
Orlando Sentinel
Palm Beach Post
People
St. Petersburg Times
South Florida Sun Sentinel
Sports Illustrated
Tampa Tribune
The Ring
USA Today

Web Sources

Baseball-Reference.com: www.baseball-reference.com
Basketball-Reference.com: www.basketball-reference.com
Black Athlete Sports Network: blackathlete.net
CBS Sports.com: www.cbssports.com
databaseOlympics.com: databaseolympics.com
ESPN: espn.go.com
Florida High School Athletic Association: www.fhsaa.org
The Florida Times-Union: jacksonville.com
Gulfstream Park: www.gulfstreampark.com
Hickok Sports: hickoksports.com
Hockey-Reference.com: www.hockey-reference.com
International Tennis Hall of Fame & Museum: www.tennisfame.com

NASCAR.com: www.nascar.com
Pro-Football-Reference.com: www.pro-football-reference.com
Professional Football Researchers Association: profootballresearchers.org
Pro Football Weekly: www.profootballweekly.com
National Museum of Racing and Hall of Fame: racingmuseum.org
Rowdy Gaines: www.rowdygaines.com
Sports Reference: www.sports-reference.com
SportsBusiness Daily: www.sportsbusinessdaily.com
Steve Carlton's Official Website: carlton32.com
USA Swimming: usaswimming.org

J. Alexander Poulton

J. Alexander Poulton is a writer, photographer and genuine sports enthusiast. He's even willing to admit he has "called in sick" during the broadcasts of major sports events so that he can get in as much viewing as possible.

He has earned a BA in English literature and a graduate diploma in journalism, and has over 20 sports books to his credit, including books on hockey, soccer, golf and the Olympics.

Ed Maloney

Ed Maloney has been a sportswriter for almost longer than he can remember. He ran the pro football and boxing channels at CBS SportsLine in Florida and eventually assumed similar duties for the official site of the San Francisco 49ers. He is a graduate of Niagara University with a degree in English, majoring in communications. He's also been a staff editor and online producer for New York/Long Island *Newsday*, and was a staff editor and feature columnist for London Publishing for 14 years. Not content just to write the news, he once made headlines when he helped snag and haul in a nine-foot, 500-pound bull shark off a dock in Tampa Bay.